SACHIN??!!

By the same author

WHAT THEY DON'T TEACH AT SCHOOL

WHAT AFTER 10+2?

SACHIN??!!

Know the God of Cricket

Vijaya Khandurie

BLUEJAY

Bluejay Books Pvt. Ltd.
A-8/76, Ist F loor
Sector 16, Rohini
Delhi 110 085
info@bluejaybooksindia.com

First published in 2014 by
Bluejay Books Pvt. Ltd.

Typeset by Eshu Graphic

Printed and bound in India

To (Late) Sh. Rameshwar Prasad Dobhal, an excellent footballer of his time who played for *Highlander Football Club* in late 50s and early 60s and enthusiastically used to recall his heroics whenever I got opportunities to meet him. Besides he was an excellent human being who loved children very much.

CONTENTS

ACKNOWLEDGEMENTS

The author did a lot of research in getting facts and records established by Sachin from various sources including the Internet. Particularly grateful to these sites: espncricinfo; Wikipedia; cricketcountry; cricketarchive; thatscricket; biography; two special issues on Sachin in *The Times of India* dated 14 November 2009 and 2 June 2012 besides a book *Sachin* by Suvam Pal. My gratitude also to my wife Manju who allowed me enough spare time to concentrate on this project.

PREFACE

Regarded as the most worshipped cricketer in the world, Sachin Tendulkar holds a number of records, unequalled by any other cricketer across the globe. When we refer to Sachin as the 'God' of cricket, we assume that a 'god' is the one whose every action is admirable. Sachin is like that: non-controversial and admired by everyone. There are many questions in the book that bear testimony to this. The phrase 'God of Cricket' was coined by none other than Matthew Hayden, former Australian captain and highest run-getter in Test matches for his country. The Little Master is so humble that once he said, "I am not God of cricket. I make mistakes, God doesn't." Sprint superstar Yohan Blake says his 'childhood hero' Sachin Tendulkar's humility has touched many people around the world and the batting legend has left an ever-lasting legacy for everyone to follow.

The present book on Sachin Tendulkar, in a quiz form, takes you to every aspect of Sachin's life from his childhood days till his retirement and the glorious cricketing days in between. Whether it was domestic cricket or a Test match or an ODI, the great maestro demonstrated his impact on the game and inspired millions of budding cricketers. His dedication towards the game of cricket is exemplary. Such great cricketers are born once in an era.

I hope the innumerable fans will recollect Sachin's memorable cricketing journey while playing through the book.

PART I

Sachin's personal life and his early phase of cricket including First Class cricket, domestic games and early professional matches

01. Sachin was born on 24 April 1973. What day of the week was it?
    (a) Sunday
    (b) Monday
    (c) Tuesday
    (d) Wednesday

02. Where was Sachin Tendulkar born?
    (a) Shree Samarth Nursing Home
    (b) Nirmal Nursing Home
    (c) Pai Nursing Home
    (d) Dr Khandeparkar Nursing Home

03. Which of these sports stars share their date of birth with Sachin Ramesh Tendulkar?
    (a) Mark Babic, Australian Olympic soccer defender
    (b) Ville Peltonen, Finnish ice hockey Olympian
    (c) Lee Westwood, English top professional golfer
    (d) All the above

04. Such people are warm, perseverant, reliable, patient, conservative, dependable, and loyal, with a strong sense of commitment and purpose. Stalwarts like Andre Agassi, Gabriela Sabatini, Guglielmo Marconi, Bertrand Russell, Madhuri Dixit, Penelope Cruz, etc., come in this category. What is the sun sign of Sachin Tendulkar which gives him these attributes?
    (a) Leo (b) Cancer
    (c) Taurus (d) Sagittarius

05. After whom did Sachin's father name him thus?
    (a) Sachin Pilgaonkar (b) Sachin Pilot
    (c) Sachin, Narvekar (d) Sachin Dev Burman

06. *Sachin* is one of the names of Lord Shiva. What is the literal meaning of the word "Sachin"?
    (a) Sensitive (b) Loving
    (c) Precious (d) All the above

07. How tall is the Little Master?
    (a) 5 ft 2 inches (b) 5 ft 3 inches
    (c) 5 ft 4 inches (d) 5 ft 5 inches

08. Sachin's mother Rajni is associated with which profession?
    (a) Real estate (b) Medical
    (c) Insurance industry (d) Marathi theatre artist

09. In which profession did Sachin's father Ramesh Tendulkar excel?
    (a) Writing (b) Theatre
    (c) Real estate (d) Medicine

10. Sachin also used to love tennis in his childhood. Which tennis great was his favourite?
    (a) Rod Laver (b) Manuel Santana
    (c) Bjorn Borg (d) John McEnroe

11. What are the names of Sachin's siblings?
    (a) Nitin and Sarita (b) Arjun and Savita
    (c) Nitin and Kavita (d) Nitin and Savita

12. What is the name of Sachin's wife?
    (a) Ankita (b) Anjali
    (c) Ananta (d) Anjani

13. Why is 24 May 1995 a landmark date in Sachin Tendulkar's life?
    (a) He met Anjali for the first time
    (b) He proposed Anjali
    (c) He was engaged to Anjali
    (d) He got married with Anjali

14. Sachin's father-in-law is a Gujarati industrialist. What is his name?
    (a) Anand Mankad (b) Anand Mistri
    (c) Anand Mehta (d) Anand Modi

15. Sachin's wife Anjali, who is about six years older to him, is a medical doctor by profession. What branch of medicine does she specialise in?
    (a) Dermatologist (b) Psychiatrist
    (c) Obstetrician (d) Paediatrician

16. Sachin and Anjali are proud parents of two children. What are their names?
    (a) Sitara and Arjun (b) Sara and Nitin
    (c) Sara and Arjun (d) Tara and Arjun

17. In which year was Sachin's daughter Sara born on 12 October?
    (a) 1996 (b) 1997
    (c) 1998 (d) 1999

18. The date "24" is something special for Sachin, because:
    (a) Sachin was born on 24 April 1973
    (b) He got married with Anjali Mehta on 24 May 1995
    (c) His son Arjun was born on 24 September 1999
    (d) All the above

19. Against which country did Sachin miss a Group A match during the 1999 Cricket World Cu in England when he had to fly back home to attend his father's funeral who had passed away on 19 May 1999?
    (a) South Africa (b) Kenya
    (c) England (d) Zimbabwe

20. Why did Sachin Tendulkar not celebrate his 38th birthday on 24 April 2011?
    (a) He was in England nursing his hamstring injury
    (b) He was strictly busy in training schedule abroad
    (c) He observed a fast in support of Anna Hazare
    (d) Due the demise of his spiritual guru Sathya Sai Baba on the same day

21. Sachin Tendulkar's son, though a teenager, is also making his mark in competitive cricket. For which team did he play his debut match in the Kanga League on 8 September 2013 against United CC and took a wicket?
(a) Shivaji Club (b) Young Parsee Club
(c) Parkophene Cricketers (d) Sportsfield *Cricket Club*

22. Who from Sachin's family said the following about Sachin's cricket love and fun: "I can be hundred percent sure that Sachin will not play for a minute longer when he is not enjoying himself. He is still so eager to go out there and play. He will play as long as he feels he can play."
(a) Ajit, his brother (b) Anjali, his wife
(c) Nitin, his brother (d) Savita, his sister

23. "The family must have been under a lot of pressure, though they didn't show that... I talk a lot of cricket with him. He has guided me throughout... We have lived our dream together. Whenever I went in to bat, I knew that mentally he was always there with me..."
Who did Sachin say this about?
(a) Vinod Kambli (b) Virender Sehwag
(c) Sachin's father (d) Ajit, Sachin's brother

24. Which, among the following statements is correct pertaining to Sachin when he played his last Test match at the Wankhede Stadium in Mumbai on 16 November 2013?
(a) The Government of India announced Bharat Ratna for him, the highest Indian civil honour
(b) He is the youngest to be awarded the Bharat Ratna
(c) He dedicated the Bharat Ratna Award to his mother
(d) All the above

25. How old was Sachin when he played cricket with a ball and a broomstick in the backyard of his house?
(a) 2 ½ years (b) 3 years
(c) 3 ½ years (d) 4 years

26. Who was the first to gift Sachin a cricket bat brought from Kashmir when he was just seven years old?
(a) Sachin's father (b) Sachin's mother
(c) Sachin's sister (d) Sachin's brother

27. Which school in East Bandra, Mumbai was Sachin a student of where he was deeply inclined to play cricket?
(a) Cardinal Gracious High School
(b) Carmel Convent Nursery School
(c) New England School of Indian Education Society
(d) Arya Vidya Mandir School

28. Name the senior secondary school where Sachin was studying as he started playing competitive cricket?
(a) J.J. Vartak School
(b) Wilson High School
(c) Dhirubhai Ambani International School
(d) Sharadashram Vidyamandir School

29. Sharadashram Vidyamandir School was famous for cricket because of its cricket coach who was instrumental in bringing Sachin to this school as he found talent in him. Who was this coach who enjoyed a reputation for cricketing excellence?
(a) Shradhnand Achrekar (b) Shashikant Achrekar
(c) Ramakant Achrekar (d) Ramakant Desai

30. Which class was Sachin a student of when he went to Shivaji Park for trials with his friend Vinod Kambli who was senior to him by a year?
    (a) VI (b) VII
    (c) VIII (d) IX

31. It's surprising that Sachin was rejected at the trials, although Vinod Kambli was selected. Who requested coach Ramakant Achrekar to give Sachin another chance, to which the coach agreed after much persuasion?
    (a) Vinod Kambli himself (b) Dilip Vengsarkar
    (c) Nitin, his brother (d) Ajit, his brother

32. About four years junior to Sachin, which famous bowler joined Sharadashram School when Sachin was in Class X and already playing for Mumbai?
    (a) Vishal Dabholkar (b) Dhaval Kulkarni
    (c) Ajit Agarkar (d) Ramesh Powar

33. Other than the under-17 Harris Shield, which is the other under-17 tournament for Mumbai schoolboys where Sachin played the competitive cricket?
    (a) Achievers Sports Club (b) Bandra Gymkhana Club
    (c) Dadar Cricket Club (d) The Giles Shield

34. In which under-17 competitive tournament in 1987 did Sachin score 1,034 runs with innings of 27*, 125, 207*, 346* and 329*?
    (a) The Giles Shield (b) The Harris Shield
    (c) K.J. Somaiya Trophy (d) Glaxo SmithKline Trophy

35. Who was the batsman at the other end in the Harris Shield match where Sachin scored a whopping 329, being in partnership with this player for 664 runs?
(a) Ajit Agarkar (b) Sairaj Bahatule
(c) Vinod Kambli (d) Milind Rege

36. How old was Sachin when he scored his first century in school level cricket in 1986?
(a) 11 years (b) 12 years
(c) 13 years (d) 14 years

37. How many triple tons did Sachin hit during his school season 1986-87, wherein he amassed more than 1200 runs?
(a) None (b) One
(c) Two (d) Three

38. Sachin's coach Shree Ramakant Achrekar used to keep a one-rupee coin on top of the stumps when Sachin was batting and gave him that coin when none of the bowlers could get him out. How many such coins did Sachin win?
(a) 11 (b) 12
(c) 13 (d) 14

39. Against which country during the 1987 World Cup at the Wankhede Stadium in Mumbai was Sachin a ball boy when he was 14 years old?
(a) New Zealand (b) South Africa
(c) Zimbabwe (d) Australia

40. For which country did Sachin play as a substitute during a One Day practice match against India at the Brabourne Stadium in 1988?
(a) Sri Lanka (b) Pakistan
(c) Bangladesh (d) West Indies

41. What was Sachin's first 'A' Division Club?
(a) Bandra XI (b) Sportsfield Cricket Club
(c) Shivaji Park (d) Young Parsee Cricket Club

42. Name the former Indian bowler who was asked by the then Indian captain Vengsarkar to bowl to Sachin in the nets in 1988?
(a) Kapil Dev (b) Ramakant Desai
(c) Paras Mhambrey (d) Ramnath Parkar

43. Who was Sachin's first captain when he started playing cricket in 'A' Division Kanga League in 1988?
(a) Raju Kulkarni (b) Kiran Mokashi
(c) Mayur Kadrekar (d) Hemant Kenkre

44. The first ball that 14-year old Sachin faced in 'A' division Kanga league against Karnataka Cricket Association in 1988 went for a six. Who was the bowler?
(a) Sharad Rao (b) Sudhakar Rao
(c) Sunil Joshi (d) Javagal Srinath

45. Who is credited for the selection of Sachin Tendulkar for the 1989 Indian tour of Pakistan?
(a) Sunil Gavaskar (b) Eknath Solkar
(c) Lalchand Rajput (d) Raj Singh Dungarpur

46. In which under-15 tournament had Sachin scored three centuries – 158*, 156 and 197 – and won the trophy for his school Shardashram Vidyamandir in 1986-87?
(a) Giles Shield
(b) Harris Shield
(c) Vijay Hazare Trophy
(d) Vijay Merchant Trophy

47. When Sachin was only 13, while playing for his school in various competitions, he scored 1028 runs in five innings in the Harris Shield. What was his highest score while remaining unbeaten?
(a) 329 (b) 336
(c) 339 (d) 346

48. At what age did Sachin make his debut for Mumbai in a First Class match in 1989?
(a) 13 years (b) 14 years
(c) 15 years (d) 16 years

49. How many runs did Sachin score while playing for Mumbai in his First Class match in 1989?
(a) 50 (b) 100
(c) 150 (d) 200

50. Against which state team did Sachin make his debut for Rest of India in Irani Trophy in 1989 and scored a century? He was the youngest to do so.
(a) Delhi (b) Karnataka
(c) Tamil Nadu (d) Gujarat

51. Who was Sachin's first captain when he played for Mumbai in Ranji Trophy and Irani Cup in 1988-89 at the age of 15?
(a) Sandeep Patil
(b) Ashok Mankad
(c) Lalchand Rajput
(d) Dilip Vengsarkar

52. In which domestic tournament did Sachin score 214 in the first innings before being stumped by Kalkumbe, bowled by Lalwani while playing for Bombay Under-19s versus Maharashtra in December 1988?
(a) Vijay Merchant Trophy
(b) Vijaya Hazare Trophy
(c) Cooch Behar Trophy
(d) Harris Shield

53. What was Sachin's score in the first innings in his debut match in Duleep Trophy in 1991? He became the first batsman to hit centuries in debut matches across the Ranji, Irani and Duleep trophies?
(a) 129
(b) 139
(c) 149
(d) 159

54. Sachin's maiden century in his debut match against Gujarat in 1988-89 Ranji Trophy was followed by a quick-fire 89 on a turning wicket against Saurashtra convinced the selectors Milind Rege and Naren Tamhane to induct him into the national team. But Sachin was disappointed when he was not called for the tour in March-May 1989. Which country was the team touring?
(a) New Zealand
(b) West Indies
(c) Sri Lanka
(d) South Africa

55. How many Ranji Trophy matches has Sachin played for Mumbai?
(a) 38 (b) 48
(c) 58 (d) 68

56. Against which team in Ranji Trophy did Sachin strike centuries in both innings (140 and 139) at the Wankhede Stadium, Mumbai in 1995 and claimed the trophy for Mumbai?
(a) Punjab (b) Haryana
(c) Uttar Pradesh (d) Rajasthan

57. Sachin played his last Ranji Trophy match against Haryana under Zahir Khan's captaincy in October 2013, scoring 79* runs. In which year had he played the only ever Ranji match against this team where he had a partnership of 96 runs with Dilip Vengsarkar?
(a) 1989 (b) 1990
(c) 1991 (d) 1992

58. While scoring 4132 runs in the Ranji Trophy, Sachin Tendulkar stands second with a batting average of 89.02. With a career batting average of 98.75, who leads the table?
(a) Vijay Merchant (b) Vijay Hazare
(c) Vijay Mehra (d) Vijay Dahiya

59. Against which team did Sachin play his Ranji Trophy 2012-13 finals and helped his team to lift the prestigious trophy?
(a) Saurashtra (b) Uttar Pradesh
(c) West Bengal (d) Karnataka

60. Against which country did Sachin Tendulkar score 331 runs with Rahul Dravid for the second wicket in 1999-2000 at the Lal Bahadur Shastri Stadium, Hyderabad and established a new record in List A Cricket?
    (a) South Africa
    (b) West Indies
    (c) New Zealand
    (d) Sri Lanka

61. How many centuries has Sachin scored in 51 innings played in 33 First Class matches on his home ground Wankhede Stadium, Mumbai including his highest (233*) with an average of 78.14?
    (a) 12 (b) 14
    (c) 16 (d) 18

62. How many centuries with an average of 147.50 has Sachin scored in the Irani Trophy at his favourite Wankhede Stadium in Mumbai?
    (a) One (b) Two
    (c) Three (d) Four

63. How many wickets has Sachin taken in First Class matches?
    (a) 51 (b) 61
    (c) 71 (d) 81

64. How many centuries has Sachin scored in List A cricket, thus occupying the number one spot?
    (a) 55 (b) 60
    (c) 65 (d) 70

65. Name the bowler who bowled Sachin out on 5 in his last Ranji Trophy match against Haryana in October 2013?
(a) Harshal Patel (b) Amit Mishra
(c) Mohit Sharma (d) Joginder Sharma

66. How many centuries has Sachin made in 489 innings of all the 309 First Class matches he has played, contributing to the whopping total of 25322 runs?
(a) 61 (b) 71
(c) 81 (d) 91

67. In which tournament played in Sharjah on 25 April 1990 was Sachin run out for the first time in ODIs after scoring 10 runs in 12 balls against Sri Lanka?
(a) Coca-Cola Cup
(b) Coca-Cola Champions Trophy
(c) Austral-Asia Cup
(d) Pepsi Asia Cup

68. At which tournament played in Headingley, Leeds on 18 July 1990 did Sachin hit his first six in ODIs when playing against England?
(a) Texaco Trophy (b) Titan Cup
(c) Future Cup (d) Wills Trophy

69. Where on 20 July 1990 in Texaco Trophy did Sachin bowl his first over, conceding 10 runs?
(a) Edgbaston, Birmingham
(b) Trent Bridge, Nottingham
(c) Headingley, Leeds
(d) Old Trafford, Manchester

70. Which combination among the following is correct in the tri-series Asia Cup final played against Sri Lanka in Eden Gardens, Kolkata on 4 January 1991?

I. Sachin equalled his previous highest ODI score of 53 runs

II. Kapil Dev took a hat-trick in the Sri Lanka innings

III. Sanjay Manjrekar was the highest scorer (75) in India's winning total of 205

IV. Mohd. Azharuddin was the man of the match for his quick-fire 54 runs

(a) I & III
(b) I & IV
(c) I, II & IV
(d) I, II, III & IV

71. Where in England did Sachin Tendulkar win the man of the match title for his 113 in 102 balls defeating Sri Lanka by 63 runs in the National Westminster Bank Series 2002 on 11 July 2002?

(a) Bristol
(b) Belfast
(c) Liverpool
(d) Cardiff

72. In the finals of which tournament played at the R. Premadasa Stadium, Colombo in September 2009, India trounced Sri Lanka by 46 runs mainly due to the *Man of the Man* Sachin's 138 runs in 133 balls?

(a) Compaq Cup
(b) Asian Cricket Council
(c) NatWest Trophy
(d) Champions League T20

73. Name the professional tournament in which Sachin hit his first ODI century in Colombo?

(a) Asia Cup
(b) Asian Test Championship
(c) Singer Cup
(d) Benson & Hedges Cup

74. In which stadium in Sri Lanka was Sachin declared man of the match award for scoring 128 runs in the Singer-Akai Nidahas Trophy Final against Sri Lanka on 7 July 1998 and won the match by 5 runs?
    (a) Sinhalese Sports Club Ground, Colombo
    (b) R. Premadasa Stadium, Colombo
    (c) Galle International Stadium, Galle
    (d) Rangiri Dambulla International Stadium, Dambulla

75. Which among the following options is true regarding Sachin's ODI century (138) in the final of the Compaq Cup on 14 September 2009 played against Sri Lanka that was instrumental in India's 46-runs win?
    (a) He was declared man of the match
    (b) He was adjudged the man of the series
    (c) Both 'a' and 'b'
    (d) None of the above

76. Whose record of most centuries (17) in One-Day Internationals did Sachin surpass when he scored his eighteenth hundred (127*) against Zimbabwe on 26 September 1998 and helped India win the match?
    (a) Brian Lara (b) Desmond Haynes
    (c) Greg Chappell (d) Allan Border

77. In a tri-series involving Australia and Sri Lanka, at which venue on 5 February 2008 did Sachin become the first and only batsman to complete 16,000 runs in ODIs?
    (a) Hobart (b) Brisbane
    (c) Sydney (d) Melbourne

78. At which place in India on 31 March 2001 did Sachin become the first batsman in ODI history to score 10,000 runs while playing against Australia?
(a) Indore (b) Kanpur
(c) Delhi (d) Ahmedabad

79. As on 24 Match 2013, during which international cricket competition did Sachin cross 18000 runs in ODIs?
(a) Tri-series in Australia
(b) Asia Cup
(c) Sir Clive Lloyd Cup
(d) Singer World Series

80. Out of 49 centuries that Sachin has hit in his ODI career, how many are at the Sharjah Cricket Association Stadium?
(a) Six (b) Seven
(c) Eight (d) Nine

81. Which among the following combination about Sachin Tendulkar is correct with respect to the Pepsi Asia Cup 1994-95 between India and Sri Lanka held at Sharjah Cricket Association Stadium in April 1995?
I. He scored a century
II. He completed 3000 runs in ODIs
III. He won the man of the match
IV. He had an opening partnership of 161 runs with Manoj Prabhakar
(a) I, II and III
(b) I, III and IV
(c) II, III and IV
(d) I, II, III and IV

82. In the Commonwealth Bank Series 2007/08 played at Bellerive Oval, Hobart on 26 February 2008, India trounced Sri Lanka by 7 wickets. Who did Sachin make a partnership of 102 runs for the second wicket with?
(a) Robin Uthappa (b) Gautam Gambhir
(c) Yuvraj Singh (d) Rohit Sharma

83. In which year did Sachin become the first overseas born player to represent English county Yorkshire at the age of 19?
(a) 1992 (b) 1995
(c) 1998 (d) 2007

84. At which venue on 11 December 1997 was Sachin stumped at 91 against England in an ODI?
(a) Sharjah (b) Perth
(c) Mirpur (d) Leeds

85. In the Asia Cup 2000 played at the Bangabandhu National Stadium, Dhaka in June 2000, India was chasing Sri Lanka's total of 276, but lost the match by 71 runs. In India's total of 205, what was the highest contribution by Sachin after facing 95 balls, excepting the second highest of 24 by Dravid?
(a) 91 (b) 93
(c) 95 (d) 97

86. How many centuries made up for his 5000 runs in Test matches with an average of 53.19? He crossed this mark during the first Test of the Asian Test Championship in 1999?
(a) 14 (b) 16
(c) 18 (d) 20

PART II

Sachin's Test Career

01. With an average of 35.83, how many runs did Sachin score in his first Test series in Pakistan in 1989-90?
    (a) 115 (b) 215
    (c) 315 (d) 415

02. Which, among the following facts, is not correct with reference to the first Test match against South Africa from 13 to 17 November 1992 at Durban?
    (a) It was the first Test match since 1970 that South Africa played at home
    (b) Omar Henry became the first non-white in the South African team
    (c) SJ Cook debuted in the match and was caught first ball by Sachin on the bowling of Kapil Dev
    (d) None of the above

03. In the historical first Test match played between India and Sri Lanka at the R. Premadasa Stadium, Colombo in August 1997, the two teams scored a total of 1,489 runs for 14 wickets. In India's score of 537 runs for 8 wickets,

three Indians scored centuries. Who, among the following is odd man out?

(a) Sachin Tendulkar (b) Mohd. Azharuddin
(c) Rahul Dravid (d) Navjot Sidhu

04. Like the first Test, the second Test match at the Sinhalese Sports Club, Colombo in India's 1997 tour also produced six centurions – three from each side. Sachin's 139 in the first innings were the fourth highest. Who with a score of 199 recorded the most runs out of both teams?

(a) Sourav Ganguly (b) Mohd. Azharuddin
(c) Sanath Jayasuriya (d) Aravinda de Silva

05. Which among the following options is incorrect with reference to the first Test match against Zimbabwe at the Feroz Shah Kotla ground, Delhi in November 2000?

(a) Sachin struck his tenth ton at home in 33 Test matches
(b) Andy Flower's 183 runs is the highest score for Zimbabwe against India
(c) Dravid-Tendulkar's partnership of 213 runs was the highest third wicket partnership for India against Zimbabwe
(d) None of the above

06. Three batsmen – Rahul Dravid, Virender Sehwag and Michael Vaughan – scored centuries in the second Test match between India and England played at Trent Bridge, Nottingham in August 2002. By how many runs did Sachin miss his century?

(a) Two (b) Four
(c) Six (d) Eight

07. When Sachin scored 193 runs in India's only innings at Headingly, Leeds, during the third Test match from 22–28 August 2002 thrashing England by an innings and 46 runs, which of the following did not occur?
   (a) It was Sachin's 99th Test match
   (b) It was Sachin's 30th Test century, just four short of Sunil Gavaskar
   (c) For the first time, Sachin, Dravid, and Ganguly scored tons in the same innings
   (d) For his achievement, Sachin was awarded the Player of the Match award

08. Which among the following options regarding Tendulkar is not true during the 4th and final Test between India and England being played at the Oval, London from 5–9 September 2002?
   (a) He played his 100th Test match, the youngest cricketer to do so
   (b) Till his 160th Test innings in this match, he scored exactly 8405 runs
   (c) At 57.96, he had the best average among the contemporary cricketers
   (d) During his 100 Test matches, he took 65 catches and 37 wickets

09. With whom did Sachin share a partnership of 255 runs while contributing 177 runs in the third Test match at Nottingham in his second tour of England in 1996, though the match ended in a draw?
   (a) Rahul Dravid
   (b) Mohd. Azaharuddin
   (c) Virender Sehwag
   (d) Sourav Ganguly

10. During the course of hitting his 31st century (176), Sachin saved the third Test match played in Kolkata in 2002 against the West Indies. Which option among the following is <u>not true</u> about it?
    (a) V.V.S. Laxman also scored a century (154*)
    (b) Tendulkar-Laxman played for a partnership of 214 runs and set a new fifth wicket record against the West Indies
    (c) Four West Indian batsmen scored centuries in their only innings of 497 runs
    (d) Shivnarine Chanderpaul equalled his highest Test score (140)

11. During the fourth and final Test against Australia in Sydney in January 2004, when Tendulkar scored an unbeaten 241 runs in the first innings, some interesting facts emerged. Which one is <u>not correct</u>?
    (a) India scored 705 for the loss of 7 wickets, their highest score so far
    (b) Steve Waugh played his 168th Test mach, his last
    (c) Anil Kumble had a match figure of 12 for 279 runs
    (d) Justine Langer scored centuries in both the innings

12. In the Multan Test in March 2004 in Pakistan, Sehwag hit 309 runs and became the first Indian to have hit a triple century. What was Tendulkar's score in the same game?
    (a) 100 (b) 196
    (c) 199 (d) 99

13. While scoring his highest score in Test matches (unbeaten 248), Tendulkar created a record for himself. What other factor(s) made this Test played against Bangladesh in Dhaka in December 2004 memorable?
    (a) Tendulkar equalled Gavaskar's record of 34 Test centuries
    (b) Tendulkar became the first Indian to score Test centuries against all the countries
    (c) Kumble bagged his 435th Test wicket to eclipse Kapil Dev's record of most wickets
    (d) All the above.

14. The second Test against Pakistan at Eden Gardens, Kolkata in March 2005 was somewhat historical, besides India's thumping win by 195 runs. Which option among the following is <u>not</u> correct?
    (a) Tendulkar joined Gavaskar, Border, Steve Waugh and Lara in completing 10,000 Test runs
    (b) Steve Bucknor became the first umpire to stand in 100 Test matches
    (c) For the second times in his career, Dravid scored centuries in both the innings
    (d) None of the above

15. Besides Tendulkar's 109 runs in the first innings, which Indian bowler opened the second innings of the second Test of the series against Sri Lanka in December 2005 and missed his century by 7 runs, helping India register an emphatic win by 188 runs?
    (a) Ajit Agarkar (b) Irfan Pathan
    (c) Anil Kumble (d) Harbhajan Singh

16. India scored a massive 610 for 3, declared in the only innings played against Bangladesh in the second Test in the series at Mirpur in 2007, defeating the hosts by an innings and 239 runs. India's first four batsmen scored centuries: Dinesh Karthik (129), Wasim Jaffer (138), Dravid (129*) followed by an unbeaten 122 by Tendulkar. Which among the following is not true?
   (a) It was India's biggest victory, as also the lead of 492 their highest ever in Tests
   (b) Tendulkar completed 11000 runs in his 137 matches
   (c) After being bowled duck in the first innings, Mohd. Ashraful (67) reached his fifty in 26 balls, the second fastest half-century in Test matches
   (d) Javed Omar became the first ever Bangladesh player to bag a 'king pair' after being dismissed for first ball duck in both the innings

17. Apart from some good batting by Australian batsmen, biased umpiring had a great hand in Aussies win in the 2nd Test in Sydney in 2007-08 series. Thanks to good batting from Tendulkar (154*) and V.V.S. Laxman (109), India took a lead of 59 runs in the first innings with a healthy score of 532 runs. What was the most significant part of this dramatic match?
   (a) Ponting equalled Steve Waugh's record of 16 consecutive wins in Tests
   (b) Kumble completed 600 Test wickets, becoming the third bowler to do so
   (c) Tendulkar hit his 38th Test century
   (d) All the above

18. Which option among the following is <u>not true</u> regarding the second Test match of the series at Mohali from 17-21 October 2008 against Australia?
    (a) A victory by 320 runs was India's biggest ever in Test matches in terms of runs
    (b) During his score of 88 runs, Tendulkar crossed a total of 12000 runs in Test matches
    (c) Amit Mishra took 7 wickets for 106 runs in his very first Test match
    (d) Gautam Gambhir scored back-to-back centuries against the Aussies

19. Mark the wrong option among the following during the first Test match in the series against South Africa played at VCA Jamtha, Nagpur from 6-9 February 2010, which India lost by an innings and 6 runs, despite Tendulkar's 91st international hundred (100)?
    (a) It was Tendulkar's third successive Test century
    (b) Hashim Amla scored his highest in Test (253*) and passed 3000 Test runs.
    (c) Jaques Kallis also scored a double ton and added 340 runs with Amla for the 3rd wicket
    (d) Dale Steyn had a haul of 10 wickets for 108, the first against India in India

20. During the 2nd Test match against South Africa at the Eden Gardens in February 2010, India levelled the series by trouncing South Africa by an innings and 57 runs, Tendulkar scoring his 47th ton (106). Among the five other century-makers from either side, who scored hundreds in both the innings (123 and 114)?
    (a) Virender Sehwag (b) V.V.S. Laxman
    (c) Alviro Petersen (d) Hashim Amla

21. Which among the following options is <u>not correct</u> with reference to the drawn Test at the Sinhalese Sports Club, Colombo from 26-30 July 2010?
    (a) India's score of 707 runs is their highest in an overseas Test
    (b) Tendulkar's 203 is his highest against Sri Lanka
    (c) Sangakkara's 219 runs is his fourth double century
    (d) Suresh Raina became the ninth Indian to score a century in his debut Test match

22. When Tendulkar scored his first century (165) in the second Test in a series against England at Chepauk Stadium, Chennai in 1992-93, which other batsman also hit a ton (106) to help India amass 560 runs, their highest total against England in India since 1951-52 at the same venue?
    (a) Vinod Kambli (b) Kapil Dev
    (c) Kiran More (d) Navjot Singh Sidhu

23. At which venue in India did Sachin score his second Test century (142) on 19 January 1994, against Sri Lanka?
    (a) Kanpur (b) Lucknow
    (c) Hyderabad (d) Nagpur

24. Which other Indian batsman scored a ton (124) when Sachin made a century (142) that helped India amass 511 runs in the first innings and defeat Sri Lanka by an innings and 119 runs in the first Test at the KD Singh Babu stadium, Lucknow in January 1994?
    (a) Navjot Singh Sidhu (b) Mohd. Azharuddin
    (c) Vinod Kambli (d) Nayan Mongia

25. By hooking a six off Walsh, Sachin completed his eighth hundred in his Test career in Nagpur on 2 December 1994. What was his score, highest so far, when he was caught by Lara off Walsh?
(a) 159 (b) 169
(c) 179 (d) 189

26. In the third and final Test match against Sri Lanka at the Wankhede Stadium, Mumbai from 3-7 December 1997, on whose bowling did Tendulkar smash two successive sixes to complete his 14th century to finally get dismissed at148 runs?
(a) C. Vaas
(b) C. Wickramasinghe
(c) K. Dharmasena
(d) R. Pushpakumara

27. The first Test of the series between Australia and India at Chepauk Stadium, Chinnai from 6-10 March 1998 is more remembered for the famous head-to-head contest between Sachin Tendulkar and Shane Warne than India's victory over the touring team by 179 runs. Warne sent Tendulkar to the pavilion for a solitary four in five balls, but in the second innings the little master thrashed Warne and remained unbeaten on 155 runs. Which of the following is <u>not correct</u> among the following? It was Sachin's:
(a) third century against Australia
(b) highest score against Australia
(c) seventh Test match against Australia
(d) highest score as a captain

28. After two straight defeats, the Aussies won the third and final Test by 8 wickets in Bengaluru on 28 March 1998 in which Sachin struck the second century of the series, which happened to be his highest against Australia. What was his score when Adam Dale bowled him?
(a) 157 (b) 167
(c) 177 (d) 187

29. In Pakistan's tour of India in 1999, Sachin scored his first century against the arch rival in the first Test at Chepauk, Chennai on 31 January 1999. He scored zero in the first innings but covered up with 136 runs in the second innings. Which Pakistani bowler got him out in both the innings?
(a) Waqar Younis (b) Wasim Akram
(c) Saqlain Mushtaq (d) Shahid Afridi

30. Which other Indian batsman scored a century (144) during the first Test in a series against New Zealand at Mohali from 10-14 October 1999 when Sachin scored an unbeaten 126, his 20th century, to propel India's score to 505 in the second innings of the drawn match?
(a) S. Ramesh (b) Vijay Bharadwaj
(c) Rahul Dravid (d) Sourav Ganguly

31. Against which country has Sachin scored his maiden double hundred (217) in his 110 innings in a Test match, played at the Sardar Patel Stadium, Motera, Ahmedabad in October-November 1999?
(a) Sri Lanka (b) New Zealand
(c) Pakistan (d) West Indies

32. Sachin Tendulkar's century (122) followed by 39 in the second innings contributed to India's win over Zimbabwe by 7 wickets in the first Test in Delhi from 18-22 November 2000. Which among the following options is not correct? It was Sachin Tendulkar's
    (a) first ever encounter against Zimbabwe in Test matches
    (b) first century against Zimbabwe
    (c) first century at the Feroz Shah Kotla ground in Delhi
    (d) 23rd Test century, next only to Gavaskar's 34

33. Other than Sachin Tendulkar (201*) and Rahul Dravid (162), which Indian batsman scored his maiden century (110) in his 3rd Test to raise the Indian total to 609 for the loss of four wickets in the drawn Test match against Zimbabwe at the VCA ground, Nagpur in November 2000?
    (a) Vijay Dahiya
    (b) Ajit Agarkar
    (c) Shiv Sunder Das
    (d) Sarandeep Singh

34. In the Nagpur Test in February 2002, India trounced Zimbabwe by an innings and 101 runs. S.S. Das and Sanjay Bangar hit centuries contributing to the huge total of 570 for the loss of seven wickets. What was Sachin's score in this match?
    (a) 150 (b) 176
    (c) 100 (d) 199

35. Trailing by 139 runs in the first innings of the third Test in a series against West Indies at the Eden Gardens, Kolkata, from 30 October to 3 November 2002, Sachin struck 176 runs to bring the match to a draw. Which of the following things did not happen during the match?
    (a) He completed 9000 runs in Test career
    (b) It was his first century at the Eden Gardens, Kolkata
    (c) With the aggregate of 212 runs in the match, he was the top scorer
    (d) He became the man of the match

36. Where on 22 December 2005 in a Test against Sri Lanka did Sachin score his 35th century (109), thus becoming the batsman with the highest number of centuries, eclipsing the record of Sunil Gavaskar?
    (a) Nagpur (b) Chennai
    (c) Delhi (d) Ahmedabad

37. Sachin contributed 109 in the 4th Test played in Nagpur on 6 November 2008 that resulted in India regaining the Border-Gavaskar Trophy by a margin of 2-1 after winning the 4th Test by 172 runs. Which was the only other player to hit a ton (102) from either side?
    (a) Sourav Ganguly (b) Virender Sehwag
    (c) Simon Katich (d) Michael Hussy

38. In response to Sachin's 41st Test century (103*), which English batsman hit a ton in both the innings (123, 108) in the first Test between India and England played in Chennai from 11-15 December 2008, which India won by 6 wickets?
    (a) P. Collingwood (b) A. Strauss
    (c) A. Cook (d) M.J. Prior

39. In the first Test match played in the series against Sri Lanka at the Sardar Patel Stadium, Motera, Ahmedabad from 16-20 November 2009, Tendulkar scored an unbeaten century (100), his eleventh. Three other Indians also hit tons (177, 110 and 110) in the drawn Test match. Who among the following is the odd one out?
(a) Rahul Dravid (b) Gautam Gambhir
(c) V.V.S. Laxman (d) M.S. Dhoni

40. Besides Tendulkar (100), who was the only other Indian to score a century (109) in the first Test match in a series against South Africa played at the VCA Stadium, Jamtha, Nagpur in February 2010, which the hosts lost by an inning and 6 runs?
(a) Murali Vijay (b) S. Badrinath
(c) M.S. Dhoni (d) Virender Sehwag

41. Murali Vijay scored 139 to contribute to India's total of 495 in the first innings of the second Test in the series against Australia in Bangalore from 9-13 October 2010 which helped India retain the Border-Gavaskar Trophy. What was Sachin's score in the two innings that played a major role in India's victory?
(a) 214 and 53* (b) 200 and 50
(c) 150 and 100 (d) 214 and 0

42. In which Test match had Sachin scored his 51st Test century, where he made 146 runs in the first innings of the third Test match between India and South Africa played at Newlands, Cape Town from 2-6 January 2011?
(a) 157th (b) 167th
(c) 177th (d) 187th

43. After scoring four tons in away matches, Sachin notched his first century at home on 12 February 1993, scoring his highest in Tests (165) at the M. A. Chidambaram Stadium, Chennai. Who was the team playing against?
    (a) West Indies (b) England
    (c) South Africa (d) Sri Lanka

44. When Sachin scored his 49th Test hundred on 11 October 2012 against Australia at Bangalore, he became the first Indian to have scored 6 Test centuries in a calendar year. Who, among the following, held the record of 5 centuries?
    (a) Sunil Gavaskar (b) Rahul Dravid
    (c) Sachin Tendulkar (d) All the above

45. While leading the Indian side in 1999-2000 tour against which country did Sachin smash 217 in a Test at Sardar Patel Stadium, Motera, Ahmedabad, thus eclipsing Sunil Gavaskar's record of 205 runs (vs West Indies) as a captain?
    (a) South Africa (b) New Zealand
    (c) Pakistan (d) Bangladesh

46. Though six batsmen scored centuries in the second Test match played at Manchester in August 1990, but the most magnificent was that of Tendulkar who rescued India from the jaws of defeat and remained unbeaten till the end of the match having batted for 224 minutes. What was his score in his first ever century against the mighty England?
    (a) 109 (b) 119
    (c) 129 (d) 139

47. In the third Test at Sydney from 2-6 January 1992, India would have won the Test but for 90 overs that were lost due to rain. Australia managed to draw it when Warne negotiated the last seven minutes at the score of 173 for the loss of 8 wickets. What is true about Sachin Tendulkar in this match?

(a) He scored 148 runs in his only innings in this Test
(b) It was his first century on Australian soil
(c) He became the youngest person to score a century in Australia
(d) All the above

48. In the first Test match played between India and Sri Lanka at the R. Premadasa Stadium, Colombo, from 2-6 August 1997, Navjot Sidhu, Sachin Tendulkar and Mohd. Azharuddin struck centuries. With 143 runs on the board, whose score was the highest?

(a) Navjot Sidhu
(b) Sachin Tendulkar
(c) Mohd. Azharuddin
(d) All scored the same

49. The consecutive century that Tendulkar made in the second Test in Colombo (139) in India's tour of Sri Lanka in 1997 was his 13th in 55 Test matches. Which Sri Lankan batsman made the same number of tons in 65 Test outings?

(a) RS Mahanama
(b) Arjuna Ranatunga
(c) MS Atapattu
(d) Aravinda de Silva

50. During the Asian Test Championship at the Sinhalese Sport Club from 24-28 February 1999 between India and Sri Lanka, which two Indian batsmen also scored centuries besides Tendulkar's 19th Test century (124) to help India score an imposing total of 518 for the loss of 7 wickets in the first innings?
(a) S. Ramesh and Sourav Ganguly
(b) Sourav Ganguly and Rahul Dravid
(c) Rahul Dravid and Mohd. Azharuddin
(d) S. Ramesh and Rahul Dravid

51. Against which country in April 2002 did Sachin Tendulkar score his 29th century (117) to equal Don Bradman's record of most centuries in Test matches in April 2002?
(a) Sri Lanka (b) England
(c) West Indies (d) Zimbabwe

52. What is Sachin Tendulkar's highest Test score against England which he made in the Leeds Test on 23 August 2002? India scored 628 in this match, their highest against England, and defeated the hosts by an innings and 46 runs?
(a) 213 (b) 203
(c) 193 (d) 183

53. At which venue in Pakistan did Sachin Tendulkar score an unbeaten 194 in their Pakistan tour in 2004, defeating the hosts by an innings and 52 runs?
(a) Lahore (b) Multan
(c) Faisalabad (d) Karachi

54. Where in Australia did Sachin score an unbeaten 241 runs, his highest score that time in the 4th Test match on 4 January 2004 in a drawn match?
(a) Melbourne (b) Adelaide
(c) Brisbane (d) Sydney

55. In the rain-affected first Test against Bangladesh at the Bir Shrestha Shahid Ruhul Amin Stadium (now known as Jahur Ahmed Chowdhury Stadium), Chittagong in March 2007, Sachin Scored his 36th ton (101). Which other Indian batsman scored a century (100) in India's first innings total of 387 for the loss of 7 wickets, declared?
(a) Wasim Jaffer (b) Dinesh Karthik
(c) Sourav Ganguly (d) M.S. Dhoni

56. In the second Test match between India and Bangladesh played in 2007 at the Sher-e-Bangla National Stadium, Bangladesh, India won by an innings and 239 runs, their biggest victory till that time. With Tendulkar (122), three other Indian batsmen also scored centuries. Which among the following is the odd one out?
(a) Dinesh Karthik (b) Wasim Jaffer
(c) Rahul Dravid (d) M.S. Dhoni

57. In an exciting finish, Australia beat India in the Sydney Test in 2007-08 series, and Tendulkar hit his 38th ton (154*). Which other Indian batsman also scored a ton (109) to raise India's total of 532 in the first innings?
(a) Rahul Dravid (b) V.V.S. Laxman
(c) Sourav Ganguly (d) Yuvraj Singh

58. Tendulkar scored his second successive Test century (153) of the Aussie tour played in the fourth and final Test at the Adelaide Oval in the 4-match Test series against Australia in January 2008. In this drawn Test, a total of 1356 runs were scored in three innings. Besides tons from Hayden (103), Ponting (140) and Clarke (118), which Indian batsman also scored a century (151) in the second innings?
(a) Anil Kumble (b) V.V.S. Laxman
(c) Virender Sehwag (d) M.S. Dhoni

59. In response to centuries hit by two New Zealanders, Ryder (102) and Vettori (118), Sachin Tendulkar scored his 42nd century (160) which helped India to their first 500 plus score in New Zealand and resulted in a 10-wicket win over the hosts in the first Test played at Seddon Park, Hamilton from 18-21 March 2009. With only 72 runs, which Indian happened to be the second highest scorer?
(a) Gautam Gambhir (b) Rahul Dravid
(c) V.V.S. Laxman (d) Zaheer Khan

60. In the first Test against Bangladesh at Zahur Ahmed Chowdhury Stadium, Bangladesh from 17-21 January 2010, Tendulkar scored his 44th Test century (105*) contributing to India's victory by 113 runs. Which other Indian batsman also scored a hundred (116) in the other innings?
(a) Virender Sehwag
(b) Gautam Gambhir
(c) V.V.S. Laxman
(d) Amit Mishra

61. Who is the other Indian to score a century (111) in the 2nd Test at the Sher-e-Bangal National Stadium, Bangladesh in 24-27 January 2010, when Tendulkar scored his 45th Test ton (143) to make India win by 10 wickets comfortably?
(a) Gautam Gambhir (b) Virender Sehwag
(c) Rahul Dravid (d) M.S. Dhoni

62. Sachin scored a double hundred (203) against Sri Lanka in the drawn Test at the Sinhalese Sports Club, Colombo in July 2010 and along with Sehwag (99) and debutant Suresh Raina (120), pushed the Indian score to 707. Prior to this, which Sri Lankan had scored a double century (219) in the Sri Lankan innings of 642 for 4 declared?
(a) T. Paranavitana (b) DPMD Jayawardene
(c) TM Dilshan (d) K. Sangakkara

63. While scoring his 51st Test hundred (146) on 4 January 2011 at Newlands, Cape Town in a drawn Test against South Africa, he became the first overseas player to have scored 5 Test centuries on South African soil. With 4 Test centuries, who were the next two?
(a) Herbert Sutcliffe and Don Bradman
(b) Don Bradman and Wally Hammond
(c) Wally Hammond and Neil Harvey
(d) Neil Harvey and Gary Sobers

64. In which year did India play against Bangladesh for the first time when Sachin scored his highest till that time (148*)?
(a) 2002 (b) 2004
(c) 2006 (d) 2008

65. At which venue in 2000 did Sachin score 117 runs against the West Indies, thus equalling Sir Donald Bradman's record of 29 Test Centuries?
(a) Kingston (b) Bridgetown
(c) Port of Spain (d) Barbados

66. Against which country in 2005 did Sachin score his 35th century to become the highest century-maker in Test cricket?
(a) Sri Lanka (b) New Zealand
(c) West Indies (d) Zimbabwe

67. Sachin has 51 Test centuries to his credit. How many of these have been scored abroad?
(a) 22 (b) 25
(c) 27 (d) 29

68. Though Sachin has scored centuries against all the Test-playing nations but name the country against whom Sachin was not able to hit a ton when away from the country?
(a) Zimbabwe (b) New Zealand
(c) West Indies (d) None of these

69. Against which country did Sachin score his last Test century away from home (146) on 4 January 2011?
(a) West Indies (b) Bangladesh
(c) New Zealand (d) South Africa

70. With whom did Sachin make his first century partnership (143 runs) in Test cricket at the Faisalabad ground in his second Test match in November 1989 for the fourth wicket when India was reeling at 33 for the loss of 4 wickets?
(a) Kapil Dev (b) Navjot Sidhu
(c) Sanjay Manjrekar (d) Mohd. Azharuddin

71. During the England tour of India in 1992-93, the tourists suffered a defeat by an innings and 15 runs in the third Test match played at the Wankhede Stadium, Mumbai, mainly due to a double century (224) by Vinod Kambli and a 194 runs partnership for the third wicket with his childhood friend Sachin Tendulkar. What was Sachin's contribution?
(a) 78 (b) 88
(c) 108 (d) 128

72. In the third Test in Sydney from 2-6 January 1992 where Tendulkar scored his first century in Australia, he was also involved in the highest ever fifth-wicket partnership (196) against Australia. Who was his partner when he got out scoring 206, his first Test double century?
(a) Kapil Dev
(b) Sanjay Manjrekar
(c) Ravi Shastri
(d) Dilip Vengsarkar

73. Tendulkar was involved in two century-partnerships, first with Navjot Sidhu (121) and then with Mohd. Azharuddin (142) in the first Test against the visitors Sri Lanka played at the KD Singh Babu Stadium in January 1994. What was Sachin's score when he was caught by Samaraweera on Anurasiri's bowling?
(a) 122
(b) 132
(c) 142
(d) 152

74. Which Indian pair scored 221 for the fourth wicket to establish a new record for India against Sri Lanka in the historical first Test at the R. Premadasa Stadium, Colombo in August 1997 in which many records were set, including Sri Lanka's 952 runs in the only innings, the highest team total in a Test match?
(a) Navjot Sidhu and Sachin Tendulkar
(b) Rahul Dravid
(c) Mohd. Azharuddin and Sachin Tendulkar
(d) None of the above

75. Who played for a partnership of 150 runs for the fifth wicket to ensure the second Test to be drawn at the Sinhalese Sports Club, Colombo in August 1997?
(a) Sachin Tendulkar and Sourav Ganguly
(b) Sachin Tendulkar and Mohd. Azharuddin
(c) Sachin Tendulkar and Rahul Dravid
(d) Nayan Mongia and Sachin Tendulkar

76. In the drawn third Test between India and Sri Lanka at the Wankhede Stadium, Mumbai in December 1997, with whom (who scored 179 runs) was Tendulkar (148) involved in a partnership of 256 runs for the fourth wicket to create a new Indian record?
(a) Rahul Dravid (b) Sourav Ganguly
(c) Navjot Sidhu (d) Mohd. Azharuddin

77. Who was Sachin's partner during the second and final Test against Australia in October 2010 while scoring his 49th Test century (214) at Bangalore in a record 308-run partnership for the third wicket, resulting in India's 2-0 series win?
(a) Rahul Dravid (100) (b) Dinesh Karthik (95)
(c) Murali Vijay (139) (d) Gautam Gambhir (99)

78. With whom did Tendulkar add 139 runs for the fourth wicket, the highest from either side, to propel India to a healthy first inning's total of 424 in the third Test against Australia at the Chinnaswami Stadium, Bengaluru in March 1998, though India lost the match by 8 wickets.
(a) Mohd. Azharuddin
(b) Rahul Dravid
(c) Sourav Ganguly
(d) V.V.S. Laxman

79. Which batsman joined Tendulkar to score 52 runs in the second innings of Chennai Test against Pakistan in January 1999 in a sixth wicket partnership of 137 runs in which Sachin was at 136, but unfortunately gave a catch to Wasim Akram on a delivery by Saqlain Mushtaq. When he was caught, India needed 17 runs for victory with 3 wickets in hand, but India lost the match by 12 runs.
(a) Sunil Joshi
(b) Nayan Mongia
(c) Anil Kumble
(d) Javagal Srinath

80. Between which two players, each scoring a hundred, a third wicket partnership of 229 runs was yielded against New Zealand at Mohali from 10 to 14 October 1999 in a drawn Test match?
(a) R. Ramesh & D. Gandhi
(b) Rahul Dravid & SachinTendulkar
(c) Sachin Tendulkar & Sourav Ganguly
(d) Nathan Astle & Stephen Fleming

81. Which Indian pair created a new record for the third wicket partnership of 249 runs in the second Test in Nagpur in November 2000 against Zimbabwe, the highest for any country against the visitors?
(a) Tendulkar – Ganguly (b) Tendulkar – Ajay Jadeja
(c) Dravid – Tendulkar
(d) Tendulkar – Shiv Sunder Das

82. While chasing down a mammoth score of 387 – the fourth highest in Test history – to beat England in the first Test in December 2008 at MA Chidambaram Stadium, Chennai, Sachin played a magnificent innings of unconquered 103 runs, hitting his 41st century. With whom did Sachin share an unbroken partnership of 163 runs to beat England by six wickets?
(a) Yuvraj Singh (b) V.V.S. Laxman
(c) Murali Vijay (d) M.S. Dhoni

83. Where in South Africa the Tendulkar-Sehwag pair accounted for the highest partnership (220) in the first Test from 3 to 6 November 2001; four of the players including Tendulkar scoring centuries?
(a) Durban (b) Port Elizabeth
(c) Pietermaritzburg (d) Bloemfontein

84. Which two players scoring centuries in the Nagpur Test made a partnership of 171 runs for the sixth wicket to enable India to register a win over Zimbabwe by an innings and 101 runs?
(a) S.S. Das & Rahul Dravid
(b) Sourav Ganguly and Sachin Tendulkar
(c) Sachin Tendulkar & Sanjay Bangar
(d) Alistair Campbell & Stuart Carlisle

85. With whom did Sachin (193) share the fourth wicket partnership of 249 runs, a record against England, during the third Test at Headingley, Leeds in August 2002, resulting in India wining by an innings and 46 runs?
(a) Rahul Dravid (b) Virender Sehwag
(c) V.V.S. Laxman (d) Sourav Ganguly

86. During the Test series between India and England in the English summer of 2002, which pair made the highest runs (249) in a four-Test series, in which the final Test was abandoned due to rain?
(a) Bangar-Tendulkar in the 2nd Test at Headingley, Leeds
(b) Vaughan-Butcher in the 4th Test at Oval, London
(c) Tendulkar-Mongia in the 2nd Test at Headingley, Leeds
(d) Tendulkar-Ganguly in the 4th Test at Oval, London

87. In India's third highest total of 675 for the loss of five wickets against Pakistan in Multan in March 2004, how many runs did Virender Sehwag (309) and Sachin Tendulkar (194*) add together for the third wicket to create a new Indian record for the third wicket partnership?
(a) 296 (b) 336
(c) 356 (d) 396

88. How many runs did Sachin Tendulkar add with Sourav Ganguly for the fourth wicket in India's total of 526 runs during which Tendulkar scored his 34th century with 248 unbeaten runs, his highest in Tests, in the match against Bangladesh in December 2004?
(a) 364 (b) 264
(c) 164 (d) 64

89. With whom does Sachin have a partnership of 6,609 runs in 136 matches, including 21 century partnerships, a world record in itself?
(a) Virender Sehwag (b) Sourav Ganguly
(c) Rahul Dravid (d) V.V.S. Laxman

90. In the fourth Test match against Australia played at the Adelaide Oval in January 2008, Tendulkar scored his 39th Test ton and established a 5th wicket partnership of 126 runs with V.V.S. Laxman (51). Which pair had the highest partnership of 210 runs in the match?
(a) Tendulkar-Laxman
(b) Kumble-Harbhajan Singh
(c) Jaques-Hayden
(d) Ponting-Clarke

91. Which Indian batsman together with Tendulkar had the highest partnership (146 runs for the fourth wicket) in the fourth Test played in Nagpur in November 2008, resulting in the hosts' victory over the Kangaroos?
(a) V.V.S. Laxman (b) M.S. Dhoni
(c) Murali Vijay (d) Kiran More

92. Among the Indian players, Tendulkar (103*) with Yuvraj Singh (85*) had the best partnership of 163 runs in the first Test between India and England played in Chennai in December 2008 which helped India to win the match by 6 wickets. Out of the two teams, which pair collectively amassed 214 runs, the highest in the match?
(a) Strauss-Bell (b) Strauss-Collingwood
(c) Strauss-Cook (d) Sehwag-Gambhir

93. Tendulkar (111) with Dhoni (90) was involved in a partnership of 172 runs for the seventh wickets, the highest by the Indians. With 230 runs on board, which South African pair made the most runs together in the first Test of the series in Centurion in December 2010 where the hosts won by an innings and 25 runs?
    (a) Kallis-Amla (b) Kallis-AB de Villiers
    (c) Smith-Kallis (d) Smith-Petersen

PART III

Sachin's One Day International (ODI) matches

01. In which Pakistani city did Sachin debut in ODIs on 18 December 1989?
    (a) Karachi (b) Lahore
    (c) Sialkot (d) Gujranwala

02. Playing at the fifth position in his very first ODI match on 18 December 1989 against Pakistan, what was Sachin's score as he was bowled by Waqar Younis and caught by Wasim Akram?
    (a) 0 (b) 1
    (c) 10 (d) 20

03. Against which country did Sachin play his 100th ODI on 24 March 1995 at Pune?
    (a) Sri Lanka (b) New Zealand
    (c) West Indies (d) South Africa

04. How many runs has Sachin scored in his ODI career beginning 1989 and ending 2012?
    (a) 17426 (b) 18426
    (c) 19426 (d) 20426

05. How many runs did Sachin score before being bowled by D. E. Malcolm in his very first ODI against England being played at Headingley, Leeds on 18 July 1990 when India trounced England by 6 wickets?
    (a) 9 (b) 19
    (c) 29 (d) 39

06. Before smashing 200 runs in 2011 at Nagpur, what was Sachin's highest score in ODIs, when he was playing his 226th match against New Zealand on 8 Nov 1999 at Hyderabad?
    (a) 175 (b) 179
    (c) 183 (d) 186

07. What was special when Sachin scored 175 runs against Australia at Hyderabad on 5 November 2009?
I. It was his highest score against Australia in an ODI
II. He completed 6000 runs in ODIs on home soil
III. He completed 17,000 runs in ODIs, a new world record
    (a) I only (b) I and II
    (c) II and III (d) I, II, and III

08. Which world record in the name of Sachin in ODIs did Sehwag Break by scoring more in a match against South Africa on 24 February 2010 at the Roop Singh Stadium, Gwalior?
    (a) Highest number of centuries
    (b) Fastest century
    (c) Unbeaten 200
    (d) Most catches taken

09. When the Master Blaster scored his 12,000 in ODIs, no other player in the world has scored more than 10,000 runs till that date. Against which nation did he achieve this milestone on 1 March 2003 with the help if his innings of 98 runs?
    (a) England (b) Pakistan
    (c) South Africa (d) New Zealand

10. Where in Pakistan on 16 March 2004 did Sachin complete 13,000 runs in ODIs while scoring 141 runs?
    (a) Lahore (b) Rawalpindi
    (c) Karachi (d) Bahawalpur

11. Against which country did Sachin establish a record of most boundaries (25) in an innings on 24 February 2010 at Gwalior?
    (a) South Africa (b) New Zealand
    (c) Bangladesh (d) Sri Lanka

12. In which year in ODIs had Sachin created a world record for most runs (1894) and most centuries (9) in a calendar year with an average of 65.31 and a strike rate of 102.15?
    (a) 1998 (b) 2000
    (c) 2002 (d) 2004

13. Against which country did Sachin complete his 15,000 ODI runs during the course of scoring 93 runs on 29 June 2007, becoming the only batsman to do so?
    (a) South Africa (b) Australia
    (c) England (d) Pakistan

14. Where in India did Sachin play his 100th ODI on 24 March 1995 during the New Zealand tour?
    (a) Indore (b) Pune
    (c) Cuttack (d) Lucknow

15. How many ODIs has Sachin played in his entire ODI matches?
    (a) 443 (b) 453
    (c) 463 (d) 473

16. What is Sachin's average in 452 innings scoring 18426 runs in 463 ODI matches?
    (a) 34.83 (b) 44.83
    (c) 54.83 (d) 64.83

17. How many times was Sachin dismissed on duck in ODI matches?
    (a) 15 (b) 20
    (c) 25 (d) 30

18. Which of the following combinations is correct as far as Sachin's performance in the ODI on 5 December 1990 against Sri Lanka being played at Nehru Stadium, Pune is concerned?

I. Scored his first half-century in ODIs
II. Took his first wicket as a bowler
III. He took two catches in the match

(a) I and II
(b) I and III
(c) II and III
(d) I, II and III

19. How was Sachin dismissed in his very first ODI being played in Gujranwala against Pakistan on 18 December 1989?
    (a) Bowled
    (b) Leg Before Wicket
    (c) Caught
    (d) Run out

20. Sachin is playing ODI matches since 1989, when he started batting on the fifth position. In which year did he open the innings for the first time, against West Indies at Port of Spain in his 44th match?
    (a) 1993
    (b) 1995
    (c) 1997
    (d) 1999

21. In the 463 ODIs that Sachin played, India won 234 and lost 200. How many times did the match end in a 'tie'?
    (a) Two
    (b) Three
    (c) Four
    (d) Five

22. How old was Sachin when he became the first batsman ever to score 200 runs in 147 balls (in a match against South Africa)?
    (a) 31
    (b) 33
    (c) 35
    (d) 37

23. How many 'Man of the Match' awards has Sachin won in his 463 ODI matches in his career, the maximum as against any other player?
    (a) 52
    (b) 62
    (c) 72
    (d) 82

24. In which year did Sachin score the most ODI runs (1894) in a calendar year?
    (a) 1996
    (b) 1998
    (c) 2000
    (d) 2002

25. Against which country has Sachin played 71 ODI matches – the most as against any other player – scoring 3077 runs with an average of 44.59?
(a) Sri Lanka (b) England
(c) Australia (d) South Africa

26. What percentage of runs for India (95,765) has Sachin contributed in his entire ODI career?
(a) 17.24 % (b) 18.24 %
(c) 19.24 % (d) 20.24 %

27. How many wickets has Sachin taken in his ODI career; it also puts him in the eleventh place among Indian bowlers?
(a) 144 (b) 154
(c) 164 (d) 174

28. Against which country was Sachin declared the player of the match for the first time in ODIs when he scored a half-century and took two wickets on 5 December 1990 in Pune?
(a) Pakistan (b) Bangladesh
(c) West Indies (d) Sri Lanka

29. How many ODIs did Sachin take to hit his first ODI century?
(a) 49 (b) 59
(c) 69 (d) 79

30. Against which country did Sachin score his first ODI century (110) in Colombo on 9 September 1994?
(a) England (b) Australia
(c) Sri Lanka (d) West Indies

31. Whose record of 183 runs did Sachin beat when the little master smashed an unbeaten 186 runs against New Zealand in an ODI on 8 November 1999?
    (a) V.V.S. Laxman (b) Vivian Richards
    (c) Rahul Dravid (d) Sourav Ganguly

32. Against which visiting country in 2009 did Sachin score 175 runs in Hyderabad while aggregating 17,000 ODI runs to become the first batsman to do so?
    (a) Australia (b) South Africa
    (c) New Zealand (d) Bangladesh

33. Sachin has most centuries in ODIs (49). Who comes next with just 30 centuries?
    (a) Herschelle Gibbs (b) Ricky Ponting
    (c) Jacques Kallis (d) Sanath Jayasuriya

34. Among the following, which interesting achievement(s) that Indians made on 15 April 1996 against Pakistan at Sharjah is correct?
    (a) Sachin scored a brilliant century
    (b) Sachin shared a second wicket partnership of 232 runs with Navjot Sidhu
    (c) It was the first instance that India scored in excess of 300 runs in ODIs
    (d) All the above

35. Out of the 49 centuries in ODIs that Sachin has scored, how many has he made away from home?
    (a) 27 (b) 28
    (c) 29 (d) 30

36. How many ODIs has Sachin played as on 16 March 2012 when he scored his hundredth 100 against Bangladesh?
(a) 442 (b) 452
(c) 462 (d) 472

37. Sachin was the first ever batsman to score a double hundred (200* against South Africa in Gwalior in February 2010) in the history of ODI cricket while playing against South Africa in 2009-10. Till then what was the highest score established by Charles Coventry as well as Saeed Anwar?
(a) 198 (b) 196
(c) 194 (d) 192

38. How many centuries has Sachin scored in the calendar year 1998, most by any other?
(a) Six (b) Seven
(c) Eight (d) Nine

39. Against which cricketing nation did Sachin score his 9th century (110*) away from home on 28 August 1996, when India lost the match?
(a) Bangladesh (b) Zimbabwe
(c) England (d) Sri Lanka

40. Against which country did Sachin score his first ODI century (112*) in Sharjah on 9 April 1995 which India won?
(a) Sri Lanka (b) Pakistan
(c) Kenya (d) Scotland

41. What is so special about Sachin's 15th ODI century (134) played against Australia in 1998 which India won? It was his:
(a) birthday on that day (b) first century at Sharjah
(c) third consecutive ton (d) highest score till that time

42. At which stadium did India lose the ODI match for the first time (vs Sri Lanka) at home on 2 March 1996, despite Sachin's brilliant innings of 137?
(a) IPCL Sports Complex Ground, Vadodara
(b) Barabati Stadium, Cuttack
(c) Feroz Shah Kotla, Delhi
(d) M. Chinnaswamy Stadium, Bangalore

43. Against which non-Test-playing country did Sachin hit a ton (127*) for the first time in ODIs on 18 February 1996 at Barabati Stadium, Cuttack?
(a) East Africa (b) Kenya
(c) Ireland (d) Canada

44. At which stadium has Sachin played most times (7) in ODIs while scoring centuries each time?
(a) Sinhalese Sports Club Ground, Colombo, Sri Lanka
(b) Wankhede Stadium, Mumbai, India
(c) R. Premadasa Stadium, Colombo, Sri Lanka
(d) Sharjah Cricket Association Stadium, Sharjah

45. What was Sachin's score when he played his 49th and last ODI century on 16 March 2012 at Shere-e-Bangla National Stadium, Dhaka against the host team Bangladesh?
(a) 114 (b) 124
(c) 134 (d) 144

46. How many times did Sachin remain not out in his 49 ODI centuries?
(a) 12 (b) 18
(c) 22 (d) 26

47. Who was Sachin's opening partner when he scored his first ODI century (110) before Craig McDormitt got him bowled, against Australia on 9 September 1994 at R. Premadasa Stadium, Colombo?
(a) Navjot Singh Sidhu (b) M. Prabhakar
(c) Nayan Mongia (d) Ajay Jadeja

48. In an exciting finish, Sachin scored his second hundred (115) and added 144 runs for the first wicket with Manoj Prabhakar (74), helping India win the match against New Zealand by 7 wickets with 11 balls remaining. At which venue was this ODI played on 28 October 1994?
(a) Baroda (b) Ahmedabad
(c) Gwalior (d) Jaipur

49. At which neutral venue did Sachin score his ODI century (112) for the first time on 9 April 1995?
(a) Pedang (b) Toronto
(c) Sharjah (d) Kuala Lumpur

50. Where on 11 November 1994 did Sachin make his first ODI century against West Indies (105 runs), thus helping India to register the win by just 5 runs and earning the Player of the Series Award?
(a) Delhi (b) Lucknow
(c) Indore (d) Jaipur

51. What was the mode of Sachin's dismissal when he scored his first century (100) against Pakistan on 5 April 1996 at the neutral venue in Singapore, despite India loosing the match by 8 wickets?
(a) Caught (b) Stumped
(c) LBW (d) Run out

52. Which other Indian also scored a century (153 runs) when Sachin scored his the then highest unbeaten 186 on 9 November 1999 against South Africa at the LBS Stadium, Hyderabad in India's massive score of 376 for the loss of two wickets, defeating the visitors by 174 runs?
(a) Sourav Ganguly (b) Rahul Dravid
(c) Ajay Jadeja (d) Vijay Bharadwaj

53. What was the breath-taking result in the penultimate ball when Sachin scored 146, almost half of India's total of 286 in an ODI match against Zimbabwe on 8 December 2000 played at the Barkatullah Khan Stadium, Jodhpur?
(a) India won by 1 wicket
(b) India won by 1 run
(c) Zimbabwe won by 1 wicket
(d) Zimbabwe won by 1 run

54. With whom did Sachin have the second-wicket partnership of 194 runs when Sachin struck his highest ODI score (200*) on 24 February 2010 against South Africa played at Captain Roop Singh Stadium, Gwalior?
(a) K.D. Karthik (b) Virender Sehwag
(c) Rahul Dravid (d) M.S. Dhoni

55. In which year did Sachin score a century (105*) in ODIs against England at Chester-le-Street without yielding any result?
    (a) 1996 (b) 1998
    (c) 2000 (d) 2002

56. How many Test hundreds had Sachin scored before his first ODI century (110) on 9 September 1994 against the Aussies played at the R. Premadasa Stadium, Colombo?
    (a) Four (b) Five
    (c) Six (d) Seven

57. From 1992 till the 2007 World Cup tournaments, Tendulkar has scored the most runs (2278). Who comes next with 1743 runs?
    (a) Matthew Hayden (b) Mahela Jayawardene
    (c) Allan Border (d) Ricky Ponting

58. Ricky Ponting has scored the second highest number of centuries (five in number) in the six World Cup tournaments. Who tops the list with six centuries to his credit?
    (a) Scott Styris (b) Martin Crowe
    (c) Sachin Tendulkar (d) Sourav Ganguly

59. With 21 half-centuries in 11 innings, Tendulkar tops the list in the World Cup matches. Way behind him, who comes next with 11 fifties to his credit?
    (a) Brian Lara
    (b) Ricky Ponting
    (c) Chris Gayle
    (d) Mohd. Azharuddin

60. In how many innings had Tendulkar scored 283 runs at an average of 47.16 with 3 fifties in his first World Cup in 1992?
    (a) Six (b) Eight
    (c) Ten (d) Twelve

61. Against which country did Tendulkar score his first World Cup century (unbeaten 127 in 138 balls) on 18 February 1996 in Barabati Stadium, Cuttack during the 1996 Wills World Cup?
    (a) West Indies (b) Australia
    (c) Kenya (d) Sri Lanka

62. How many runs did Sachin score in the 1996 Wills World Cup, most by any other batsman?
    (a) 513 (b) 523
    (c) 533 (d) 543

63. What was Sachin's score in a World Cup match being played against Australia in Mumbai on 27 February 1996 when Sachin was stumped off a wide ball by Ian Healy?
    (a) 60 (b) 70
    (c) 80 (d) 90

64. In the World Cup opening game against Bangladesh in 2011, Sachin became the most capped player in ODIs. Whose tally of 444 matches did Sachin surpass?
    (a) Brian Lara
    (b) Allan Border
    (c) Viv Richards
    (d) Sanath Jayasuriya

65. In which World Cup was Sachin adjudged the Man of the Tournament at the end of World Cup finals?
(a) 1996 (b) 1999
(c) 2003 (d) 2007

66. In which two editions of the World Cup does Sachin hold a world record of 4 consecutive fifties?
(a) 1992 and 1995-96
(b) 1995-96 and 1999
(c) 1995-96 and 2002-03
(d) 2002-03 and 2007

67. At which venue did Sachin Tendulkar pass his previous highest score of 127 in ODIs by scoring 137 runs against Sri Lanka in the World Cup on 2 March 1996?
(a) Gaddafi Stadium, Lahore
(b) Wankhede Stadium, Mumbai
(c) Feroz Shah Kotla, Delhi
(d) Eden Gardens, Kolkata

68. In the semi-finals of the World Cup at the Eden Gardens, Kolkata on 13 March 1996 against Sri Lanka, India was chasing Sri Lanka's score of 251 runs and at one stage were 98 for the loss of 2 wickets. The batting order collapsed all of a sudden and the Indian was reeling at 120/8 in 34.1 overs. Due to the crowds' hooliganism, the match was abandoned and Sri Lanka won the match by default. What was Tendulkar's contribution to India's total of 120?
(a) 45 (b) 55
(c) 65 (d) 75

69. Against which nation did Sachin score an unbeaten 152 runs, his highest score in the World Cup?
    (a) Ireland (b) East Africa
    (c) Namibia (d) Zimbabwe

70. Where did Sachin score his last century (111) in the sixth edition of the World Cup against South Africa on 12 March 2011?
    (a) Kolkata (b) Nagpur
    (c) Bangalore (d) Mohali

71. In a league match, India defeated Sri Lanka by a whopping 157 runs curtsey 183 by Ganguly and 145 by Dravid in a record partnership of 318 runs on 19 May 1999 in Taunton during the World Cup. Who clean bowled Sachin for 2 runs scored in just 3 balls?
    (a) M. Muralitharan
    (b) Sanath Jayasuriya
    (c) C. Vaas
    (d) Eric Upashantha

72. What is Sachin's average of scoring runs in World Cup matches he has played?
    (a) 52.95 (b) 54.95
    (c) 56.95 (d) 58.95

73. Against which country did Sachin score 140 runs in 101 balls in a Group A match on 23 May 1999? He was also declared Player of the Match?
    (a) Kenya (b) England
    (c) Sri Lanka (d) South Africa

74. Whose was the first ever catch that Sachin took in his first appearance in a World Cup on 22 February 1992 played at WACA Ground, Perth, against England?
(a) Ian Botham
(b) Graham Gooch
(c) Graem Hick
(d) Derek Pringle

75. Which two batsmen from India had already scored centuries in World Cup before Sachin scored his first century (127*) on 18 February 1996 against Kenya at Cuttack?
(a) Navjot Sidhu and Kapil Dev
(b) Kapil Dev and Sunil Gavaskar
(c) Sunil Gavaskar and Dilip Vengsarkar
(d) Dilip Vengsarkar and Kapil Dev

76. Scoring an unbeaten 54 runs and capturing a wicket against which country did Sachin earn his first ever Player of the Match trophy in the 1992 World Cup?
(a) Pakistan
(b) Zimbabwe
(c) Sri Lanka
(d) England

77. In the 2011 World Cup, the 11th match ended in a 'tie' between India and England played at the M. Chinnaswamy Stadium, Bangalore on 27 February 2011 where Sachin scored 120 runs with 5 sixes. How many runs did each side score?
(a) 308 (b) 318
(c) 328 (d) 338

78. In an exciting finish in a League match of the 2011 World Cup played at the Vidarbha Cricket Association Stadium, Nagpur on 12 March 2011, which country defeated India by 3 wickets with just 2 balls remaining despite Sachin's flawless 111 runs?
(a) Australia (b) Bangladesh
(c) South Africa (d) Ireland

79. Where in India did Sachin win the Player of the Match title after scoring 85 runs in the second semi-final against Pakistan on 30 March 2011, defeating the opponent by 29 runs?
(a) Nagpur (b) Ahmedabad
(c) Mohali (d) Delhi

80. How many runs did Sachin make in his last World Cup appearance when India became champions trouncing Sri Lanka by 6 wickets at the Wankhede Stadium on 2 April 2011?
(a) 8 (b) 18
(c) 28 (d) 38

81. In which edition of the Indian Premier League did Tendulkar participate for the first time as captain of the Mumbai Indians playing against Chennai Super Kings?
(a) IPL-1, 2008 (b) IPL-2, 2009
(c) IPL-3, 1910 (d) IPL-4, 1911

82. In the first Indian Premier League (IPL-1) in 2008, how many half-centuries did Tendulkar score in 7 matches?
(a) One (b) Two
(c) Three (d) Four

83. In which edition of the IPL did Tendulkar win the *Orange Cap* for scoring the most runs (618) in the tournament including 5 fifties?
(a) IPL-1, 2009 (b) IPL-2, 2010
(c) IPL-3, 1911 (d) IPL-4, 1912

84. In which edition of the IPL did Tendulkar score his only century (unbeaten 100)?
(a) IPL-1, 2009 (b) IPL-2, 2010
(c) IPL-3, 1911 (d) IPL-4, 1912

85. How many half-centuries (including a ton) has Tendulkar scored in his total of 78 matches played in all the editions of the Indian Premier League put together?
(a) 10 (b) 12
(c) 14 (d) 16

86. Which is the only edition of the IPL in which Tendulkar bowled 6 overs conceding 58 runs without taking a wicket?
(a) IPL-1, 2009 (b) IPL-2, 2010
(c) IPL-3, 1911 (d) IPL-4, 1912

87. In the fourth edition of the Indian Premier League 2011, Tendulkar was the second highest scorer among the Indian batsmen with 553 runs, including a century. Who won the *Orange Cap* for aggregating the most runs (608)?
(a) Shaun Marsh
(b) Virat Kohli
(c) Chris Gayle
(d) Michael Hussy

88. To whom did Sachin hand over the captaincy of his team in the fifth edition of the IPL Tournament in 2012?
    (a) Rohit Sharma (b) Mark Baucher
    (c) Dwayne Bravo (d) Harbhajan Singh

89. With an average of 34.83, how many runs has Sachin scored in 78 IPL matches?
    (a) 2134 (b) 2234
    (c) 2434 (d) 2534

90. Which IPL T-20 team trounced the runners-up Mumbai Indians in the first outing at the Wankhede on 21 April 2011 by a huge eight-wicket margin, though the skipper Sachin Tendulkar scored his first Indian Premier League century?
    (a) King's XI Punjab (b) Delhi Daredevils
    (c) Kochi Tuskers Kerala (d) Royal Challengers Bangalore

91. How many times did Sachin go out for duck in his 78 appearances for Mumbai Indians in six editions of the Indian Premier League?
    (a) Once (b) Twice
    (c) Thrice (d) Four

92. For which role was Sachin signed for a sum of US$ 1,121,250 in the inaugural Indian Premier League Twenty 20 competition in 2008?
    (a) Being captain of the Mumbai Indians
    (b) Being a member of the Football club Mumbai FC
    (c) As a gesture of gratefulness by the owners Reliance Industries
    (d) As an Icon Player

93. While playing an IPL fixture at Port Elizabeth, South Africa, against which team did Sachin smash 68 runs, seen as one of his best innings in IPL?
(a) Deccan Chargers, Hyderabad
(b) Kings XI Punjab
(c) Delhi Daredevils
(d) Kolkata Knight Riders*

94. How many catches has Sachin taken in his IPL career?
(a) 23 (b) 25
(c) 27 (d) 29

95. Which, among the following statements, is <u>incorrect</u> so far as Sachin's performance in the 3rd edition of IPL in 2010 is concerned?
(a) He scored 63 runs in just 32 balls
(b) Mumbai Indians reached the finals for the first time mainly due to his performance
(c) He captured the *Orange Cap* by scoring 618 runs in 14 outings
(d) None of these

96. Who got Sachin out for 72, caught by Dhoni, in what was his best innings while playing against Chennai Super Kings in 2010 IPL when Mumbai Indians just needed 9 runs off 10 balls, which his team easily achieved?
(a) Lakshmipathi Balaji
(b) Albie Morkel
(c) Suresh Raina
(d) Jacob Oram

97. Against which team did Sachin win another Man of the Match title for his unbeaten 89 in 2010 edition of the IPL, one of his most memorable innings in IPL?
(a) Kolkata Knight Riders
(b) Deccan Chargers, Hyderabad
(c) Rajasthan Royals
(d) Kings XI, Punjab

98. Though Kochi Tuskers Kerala defeated Mumbai Indians in an IPL fixture in 2010 edition, however Sachin got much applaud from the crowd for his unbeaten 100 made in 66 balls. In how many balls did he score his second fifty?
(a) 19 (b) 21
(c) 23 (d) 25

99. Where did Sachin score 48 runs in 28 balls against the Kolkata Knight Riders in his sixth and last edition of the IPL Tournament 2013 and helped his team post 170 runs?
(a) Mumbai (b) Delhi
(c) Chandigarh (d) Cuttack

100. In the second IPL Tournament in 2009, Tendulkar scored 364 runs altogether in 13 matches, with two fifties. Who topped the list by aggregating 552 runs in 12 outings with 5 fifties?
(a) Adam Gilchrist
(b) Tilakaratne Dilshan
(c) AD de Velliers
(d) Matthew Hayden

101. The third edition of the Indian Premier League was the first season when both teams in the final were captained by Indians, one of them was Sachin Tendulkar for Mumbai Indians. Who was the other?
(a) Sourav Ganguly (b) M.S. Dhoni
(c) Gautam Gambhir (d) Anil Kumble

102. In Sachin's T20 farewell match, what was his contribution in a total of 202/6 runs for Mumbai Indians when they trounced Rajasthan Royals by 33 runs in the finals of the fifth edition of the Champions League being played at Feroz Shah Kotla, Dehli on 6 October 2013?
(a) 15 (b) 25
(c) 35 (d) 45

103. What was the winning percentage of Mumbai Indians whenever Sachin got out for a duck?
(a) 25% (b) 50%
(c) 75% (d) 100%

104. In his first ever appearance in the Champions League Trophy on 10 September 2009 played at the New Wanderers Stadium, Johannesburg, Sachin was leading the Mumbai Indians against Kings XI Punjab. What was Sachin's score out of the team total 177/6 before being bowled?
(a) 0 (b) 49
(c) 69 (d) 99

PART IV

Awards, Accolades Firsts, Praise and Records

01. Highlight the first occasion when Sachin won the Man of the Match title in a Test match?
    (a) On 23 November 1989 against Pakistan at Faisalabad
    (b) On 9 December 1989 against Pakistan at Sialkot
    (c) On 9 February 1990 against New Zealand at Napier
    (d) On 9 August 1990 against England at Manchester

02. For which outstanding performance Sachin received his first Man of the Match Award on 9 August 1990 against England at Manchester? For
    (a) Scoring 68 runs in the 1st innings
    (b) Taking two catches
    (c) Scoring an unbeaten century (119) in India's second innings
    (d) All the above

03. Where in India did Sachin win the Player of the Match title against Pakistan for the first time for scoring 136 runs and taking 3 wickets in the first Test from 28-31 January 1999, though India lost the match?

(a) Chepauk Stadium, Chennai
(b) Feroz Shah Kotla Stadium, Delhi
(c) Wankhede Stadium, Mumbai
(d) Green Park Stadium, Kanpur

04. For scoring 446 Test runs in three matches, Sachin was awarded Man of the Series for Border-Gavaskar Trophy played in India during 1997-98 season. How many tons did Sachin hit in five innings?
(a) One (b) Two
(c) Three (d) Four

05. Scoring an unbeaten 54 runs and capturing a wicket against which country did Sachin earn his first ever Player of the Match title in the 1992 World Cup?
(a) Pakistan
(b) Zimbabwe
(c) Sri Lanka
(d) England

06. Against which country was Tendulkar awarded the Player of the Match for his match-winning score of 70 runs, the most by any on 21 February 1996 in the 1996 Wills World Cup?
(a) Zimbabwe (b) Sri Lanka
(c) West Indies (d) Australia

07. How many Man of the Match titles does Sachin Tendulkar have to his credit?
(a) 52 (b) 62
(c) 72 (d) 82

08. Sachin Tendulkar has the distinction of having won Man of the Match titles in ODIs against all the Test playing nations (the maximum 11 against Australia), but has not against some associate members recognised by the ICC. Identify them.
    (a) Bermuda (b) United Arab Emirates
    (c) Netherlands (d) All the above

09. Where was Sachin awarded the Man of the Match title the most times (4) in Test matches against four different countries?
    (a) SCG, Sydney (b) Wankhede, Mumbai
    (c) Chepauk, Chennai (d) Eden Gardens, Kolkata

10. Sachin Tendulkar tops the list to have won most Man of the Match (62) titles in 463 ODIs. With 48 awards in 445 innings, who stands second?
    (a) Vivian Richards (b) Sanath Jayasuriya
    (c) Ricky Ponting (d) Jacques Kallis

11. For which outstanding effort was Sachin declared the Player of the Series during England's tour of India in 2001? He scored:
    (a) A century in the first Test
    (b) Two centuries in the series
    (c) Most runs (307) in the series
    (d) A century, took 4 catches and a wicket

12. Against which touring team was Sachin voted the Player of the Series in the 2-match Test series in May 2007 for his back-to-back centuries, 4 catches and 3 wickets?
    (a) Bangladesh (b) West Indies
    (c) England (d) Pakistan

13. In which year was Sachin Tendulkar adjudged the Man of the Tournament in the ICC World Cup for scoring the most runs (673) and taking two wickets?
    (a) 1996 (b) 1999
    (c) 2003 (d) 2007

14. In which season of the Border-Gavaskar Trophy series was Sachin Tendulkar chosen as the Player of the Series for the first time for his 446 runs in three matches with 2 centuries, a fifty, one wicket and two catches?
    (a) 1997-98 (b) 1999-2000
    (c) 2001-02 (d) 2003-04

15. Which two other countries were involved in the Singer Tri-series when Sachin was declared the Man of the Series for the first time in 1994?
    (a) Australia and New Zealand
    (b) New Zealand and South Africa
    (c) South Africa and Sri Lanka
    (d) Sri Lanka and Australia

16. Which of the following statements is <u>not true</u> about Sachin's achievements? He holds the world record of the most number of Man of the ...?
    (a) Match titles in ODIs (b) Match titles in Tests
    (c) Series titles in ODIs (d) Match titles in World Cup

17. In which year did Sachin receive his last Man of the Series title for his 204 runs including a ton in two-match ODI series during the tour of South Africa to India?
    (a) 2008-2009 (b) 2009-10
    (c) 2010-11 (d) 2011-12

18. While taking his very first wicket in ODIs against Sri Lanka on 5 December 1990, for which effort did Sachin win the Man of the Match title?
    (a) For his controlled bowling analysis: 9-039-2
    (b) For good fielding while taking 2 difficult catches
    (c) For scoring 53 runs, helping India to win
    (d) All the above

19. How many times has Sachin won the Man of the Match title in his 45 outings in the World Cup?
    (a) 9 (b) 10
    (c) 11 (d) 13

20. Sachin made his ODI debut on 18 December 1989 at Municipal Stadium, Gujranwala and was dismissed at duck when Wasim Akram took the catch on Waqar Younis's ball. How many balls did he face?
    (a) 1 (b) 2
    (c) 3 (d) 4

21. In which Test match of the South African tour of 1992-93 did Sachin score his first century (111) against South Africa, and fourth of his career?
    (a) 1st Test at Durban
    (b) 2nd Test at Johannesburg
    (c) 3rd Test at Port Elizabeth
    (d) 4th Test at Cape Town

22. Where on 1 December 1990 did Sachin play his first ODI in India, equalling his previous highest of 36 runs in 22 balls when India defeated Sri Lanka by 19 runs?
    (a) Mumbai (b) Delhi
    (c) Jaipur (d) Nagpur

23. On which ground in India did Sachin strike his first ODI fifty (53 runs off 41 balls) while playing against Sri Lanka on 5 December 1990?
(a) Feroz Shah Kotla, Delhi
(b) Nehru Stadium, Pune
(c) Wankhede Stadium, Mumbai
(d) Vidarbha Cricket Association Ground, Nagpur

24. Who was Sachin's first victim (clean bowled) in ODIs as a bowler on 5 December 1990 while playing against Sri Lanka at Nehru Stadium, Pune?
(a) R.S. Mahanama
(b) D. Ranatunga
(c) M.S. Atapattu
(d) R.J. Ratnayake

25. At the age of 16 years and 205 days, Sachin became the youngest cricketer to play at the Test level for India against Pakistan in 1988-89. Where was this match played?
(a) Lahore
(b) Karachi
(c) Gujranwala
(d) Faisalabad

26. Where did Sachin play his first Test match against Sri Lanka on 23-27 November 1990 where India won by an innings and 8 runs?
(a) IPCL Sports Complex Ground, Vadodara
(b) Sawai Mansingh Stadium, Jaipur
(c) Sector 16 Stadium, Chandigarh
(d) Barabati Stadium, Cuttack

27. Tendulkar's ODI career changed when he moved from the middle order to open the innings. Against which country did he do so for the first time on 27 March 1994 while scoring 82 runs off 49 balls?
(a) New Zealand
(b) South Africa
(c) West Indies
(d) Sri Lanka

28. Where did Sachin score his first Test century (unbeaten 104) against Sri Lanka in 1993 when India crashed Sri Lanka by 235 runs in the second Test?
(a) Tyronne Fernando Stadium, Moratuwa
(b) R Premadasa Stadium, Colombo
(c) Sinhalese Sports Club Ground, Colombo
(d) Asgiriya Stadium, Kandy

29. Sachin Tendulkar was the first batsman to reach 200 runs in an innings in the World Cup. Who was the second?
(a) McCullum
(b) Jacques Kallis
(c) Graem Smith
(d) Virender Sehwag

30. In which stadium did India win a Test match involving Sachin's ton (165) for the first time (vs England) in February 1993?
(a) M. A. Chidambaram Stadium, Chennai
(b) K. D. Singh Babu Stadium, Lucknow
(c) M. Chinnaswamy Stadium, Bangalore
(d) Eden Gardens, Kolkata

31. Sachin is the first cricketer to be nominated to the Rajya Sabha. On being nominated to the Upper House of the Parliament, which great Indian footballer remarked, "Sachin will do a great job if he becomes an MP in the Rajya Sabha. We need honest people like him."?
(a) Chuni Goswami (b) P.K. Bannerjee
(c) Baichung Bhutia (d) Syed Rahim Nabi

32. What was the match performance of Sachin in Test matches when he was declared the Man of the Match for the first time (against England at Old Trafford in 1990)?
(a) Scoring 68 runs in the first innings
(b) Scoring 119 runs in the second innings
(c) Taken two vital catches
(d) All the above

33. Which among the following options is <u>not correct</u> about Sachin Tendulkar? He is the first cricketer to
(a) Reach 10,000 runs in ODIs
(b) Have scored over 100 innings of 50+ runs in ODIs
(c) Score a century and capture four wickets in the same ODI
(d) None of the above

34. Which among the following options is correct about Sachin Tendulkar? He is the only cricketer to:
(a) Have made three scores of 175 or more in ODIs
(b) Score a century for Indian captaincy on ODI debut
(c) Be in top 10 ICC Batsmen ranking for 10 years in Tests
(d) All the above

35. Sachin Tendulkar was the first cricketer to be awarded the prestigious Rajiv Gandhi Khel Ratna award in 1997-98. Who was the second cricketer to be awarded the same in 2007-08?
(a) Rahul Dravid (b) M.S. Dhoni
(c) Sourav Ganguly (d) None of the above

36. Sachin is the only player in the world who has scored 96 half-centuries in ODIs. Who is the next with 85 half-tons?
(a) Inzamam-ul-Haq (b) Jacques Kallis
(c) Rickey Ponting (d) Sanath Jayasuriya

37. Sachin was 28 years 5 months old when he played his 100th Test match from 5-9 September 2002, scoring his 34th half century (54) in the only innings of the 4th Test against England, and became the youngest Test player in the world to play a century of Test matches. Where was this match played?
(a) Edgbaston, Birmingham
(b) The Oval, London
(c) Trent Bridge, Nottingham
(d) Old Trafford, Manchester

38. At which venue did Sachin become the first person to complete 12,000 runs during his 88-run knock on the opening day of the second Test match against Australia on 17 October 2008?
(a) Mohali (b) Gwalior
(c) Jaipur (d) Ahmedabad

39. In how many innings did Sachin cross 15,000 runs while playing against West Indies in 2011-12 series at Feroz Shah Kotla, Delhi?
(a) 250 (b) 300
(c) 350 (d) 400

40. How many centuries did Sachin make in his first tour of Australia in 1991-92?
(a) Nil (b) One
(c) Two (d) Three

41. Against which country in the ODI Commonwealth Bank Tri-series did Sachin become the first and only batsman to complete 16,000 runs in ODIs on 5 February 2008 at Brisbane?
(a) New Zealand (b) England
(c) Sri Lanka (d) South Africa

42. At which ground in South Africa did Tendulkar become the first ever batsman to score his 50th Test century (111*) on 19 December 2010 while playing against South Africa?
(a) Newlands, Cape Town
(b) Old Wanderers, Johannesburg
(c) St George's Park, Port Elizabeth
(d) SuperSport Park, Centurion

43. Where in India did Sachin become the first and only cricketer to score 34,000 international runs during the 3rd Test against England on 5 December 2012?
(a) Pune (b) Bangalore
(c) Kolkata (d) Delhi

44. Which among the following statements about Sachin's first is <u>not correct</u>? He was the first batsman to hit:
    (a) 2000 fours in ODIs
    (b) 2000 fours in Tests
    (c) 4000 fours in international cricket
    (d) None of the above

45. How many half-centuries has Sachin scored in ODIs to become the first cricketer to hit most number of half-tons?
    (a) 63 (b) 73
    (c) 83 (d) 93

46. Where on 29 July 2011 against England did Sachin become the first cricketer to play 100 overseas Test matches?
    (a) Old Trafford, Manchester
    (b) Headingley, Leeds
    (c) Lord's, London
    (d) Trent Bridge, Nottingham

47. Sachin became the first batsman to aggregate 400 runs in World Cup three times. In which year did he have the highest average (87.16)?
    (a) 1996 (b) 2003
    (c) 2007 (d) 2011

48. Against which particular country does Sachin have most runs (3005) in his 67 ODIs?
    (a) Sri Lanka (b) South Africa
    (c) Australia (d) England

49. On which ground in India did Sachin Tendulkar become the highest run-scorer in the fourth innings of Test matches on 09 Nov 2011?
    (a) Feroz Shah Kotla Stadium, Delhi
    (b) Sardar Patel Stadium, Motera
    (c) Wankhede Stadium, Mumbai
    (d) MA Chidambaram Stadium, Chennai

50. Which world record has Sachin established during the match against Australia on 24 March 2011 at Sardar Patel Stadium, Motera, Ahmedabad?
    He became the first to:
    (a) Cross 18,000 runs in ODIs
    (b) Play 450 ODI matches
    (c) Cross 8,000 Test runs away from home
    (d) Cross 2,000 world cup runs

51. It is not unusual for Sachin to be out in nervous nineties. How many times has he been dismissed in nineties in Tests, the most with any batsman?
    (a) 12 (b) 15
    (c) 18 (d) 21

52. How many times has Sachin been dismissed on 99 in ODIs, which is a record in itself?
    (a) Three (b) Four
    (c) Five (d) Six

53. Against which country did Sachin become the first batsman to hit 29 Test centuries away from home on 4 January 2011, to establish a world record?
    (a) Zimbabwe (b) South Africa
    (c) New Zealand (d) Australia

54. Who is/was nearest to Sachin's record of scoring most half-centuries (96) in ODIs?
    (a) Jacques Kallis (b) Ricky Ponting
    (c) Graem Smith (d) Sanath Jayasuriya

55. How many times has Sachin scored most 1000 Test runs in a calendar year, a word record?
    (a) Three (b) Four
    (c) Five (d) Six

56. Sachin has scored centuries against every Test-playing nation in Test matches. Against which country has he scored most centuries (11)?
    (a) Pakistan (b) Australia
    (c) England (d) Sri Lanka

57. How many Test matches did Sachin play continuously for India before taking rest, a record that time?
    (a) 74 (b) 84
    (c) 94 (d) 104

58. Against which Test-playing country does Sachin hold his best Test average of 133.66?
    (a) Zimbabwe (b) New Zealand
    (c) West Indies (d) Bangladesh

59. How many runs has Sachin scored between two dismissals in 2003-04 having scored of 241*, 60*, 194* and 2 and establishing a record?
    (a) 397 (b) 497
    (c) 597 (d) 697

60. With 2016 boundaries (fours), Sachin has the most fours scored in ODIs. With 1500 hits to the rope, who comes next?
(a) Ricky Ponting (b) Adam Gilchrist
(c) Chris Gayle (d) Sanath Jayasuriya

61. How many innings has Sachin played in his 200 Test matches, most in the world?
(a) 319 (b) 329
(c) 339 (d) 349

62. In which year did Sachin make most runs in a calendar year (1894 in 33 innings), a new world record in ODIs?
(a) 1998 (b) 2000
(c) 2004 (d) 2007

63. Whose record of 19 tons of 150-plus runs did Sachin break while smashing his twentieth century against the Aussies in Bangalore on 11 October 2010?
(a) Ricky Ponting (b) Steve Waugh
(c) Brian Lara (d) Allan Border

64. How many times has Sachin opened the innings in ODI cricket, which is a record in itself?
(a) 310 (b) 320
(c) 330 (d) 340

65. How many centuries had Sachin scored before the age of 20, which happens to be a World record?
(a) 3 (b) 4
(c) 5 (d) 6

66. Sachin has scored 34,283 runs in international cricket that includes Tests, ODIs and T20 Internationals, a world record. Who comes a distant second with 27,483 runs?
(a) Vivian Richards (b) Sanath Jayasuriya
(c) Jacques Kallis (d) Ricky Ponting

67. Whom did Sachin surpass by scoring most half-centuries in Test matches during the first Test match against Australia at Melbourne Cricket Ground, on 27 December 2011?
(a) Rahul Dravid (b) Allan Border
(c) Both the above (d) None of the above

68. Against which country has Sachin played most Test matches (31)?
(a) Australia (b) England
(c) South Africa (d) Sri Lanka

69. Among Sachin's 49 ODI tons, most by any other cricketer, how many of them were scored on home grounds?
(a) 19 (b) 23
(c) 29 (d) 33

70. How many hundreds did Sachin hit while playing at the Sharjah Cricket Association Stadium, most by any other batsman?
(a) Five (b) Six
(c) Seven (d) Eight

71. How many times has Sachin reached his hundred with a six in Test matches, a world record?
(a) Five (b) Six
(c) Seven (d) Eight

72. How many times has Sachin featured in India's victory in Test matches, most by any other Indian?
(a) 40 (b) 50
(c) 60 (d) 70

73. When Sachin had scored 33 runs in the second Test at Johannesburg in 1992, he set an Indian record of being the youngest batsman at 19 years 217 days to reach 1000 Test runs. Who at 21 years 27 days had the previous record?
(a) Ravi Shastri (b) Mansur Ali Khan Pataudi
(c) Kapil Dev (d) Sunil Gavaskar

74. Sachin has created a new record by becoming the first and only cricketer to score a century (141) and take 4 wickets for 38 runs in the same ODI. At which venue did he achieve this feat against Australia on 28 October 1998?
(a) Sydney (b) Sharjah
(c) Dhaka (d) Nagpur

75. Whose record of 32 Test centuries did Sachin Tendulkar break when he scored an unbeaten 194 runs, his 33rd Test century, against Pakistan on 29 March 2004 in Multan?
(a) Mark Waugh (b) Steve Waugh
(c) Ricky Ponting (d) Brian Lara

76. Sachin has a record of scoring most centuries (49) in ODIs. How many of these are 150 plus, a world record?
(a) Four (b) Five
(c) Six (d) Seven

77. In how many Test matches did Sachin complete 4000 runs during the third Test match against Sri Lanka at the Wankhede Stadium, Mumbai in December 1997? He made his 14th century during the same match?
(a) 38 (b) 48
(c) 58 (d) 68

78. Against which country did Tendulkar complete his 5000 Test runs in a riot-affected match in Kolkata in February 1999 at the Eden Gardens, when he was declared run out for two runs and the match was disrupted for hours in The Asia Cup Championship?
(a) Bangladesh (b) Sri Lanka
(c) Pakistan (d) New Zealand

79. At which venue did Sachin Tendulkar cross his 7500 Test runs during his innings of 176 runs against Zimbabwe in 2002?
(a) Nagpur (b) Ahmedabad
(c) Delhi (d) Bangalore

80. Which land mark did Sachin create when India trounced Pakistan by 195 runs in the second Test at Eden Gardens, Kolkata in March 2005?
(a) He hit two half-centuries in the same Test for the first time
(b) His performance led India to their first victory over Pakistan in Kolkata in six outings
(c) He completed 10,000 runs in Test cricket
(d) He completed 200 innings in Test matches

81. In the 4th ODI match against Sri Lanka at the Sinhalese Sports Club Ground, Colombo on 24 August 1997, India lost the match by 9 runs. But which milestone did Sachin Tendulkar achieve?
   (a) He captured 50 wickets in ODIs
   (b) He scored his first 150 runs against Sri Lanka
   (c) He took the 50th catch in ODIs
   (d) He completed 5500 runs in ODIs

82. While scoring 241* and 60* runs in the drawn Test against Australia in the Sydney Cricket ground in January 2004, which of the following records were not made by Sachin?
   (a) It was his 32nd Test century equalling Steve Waugh's record
   (b) He passed the 9000 runs mark in Test cricket, becoming the fourth person to do so
   (c) Up to this date, this was his highest score in first class matches also
   (d) At the end of the series after this match, he was declared the Player of the Series

83. In the drawn 3rd Test against Sri Lanka at the Wankhede Stadium, Mumbai (3-7 December 1997), some record(s) was/ were established. Tick the correct one.
   (a) Ganguly posted his highest Test runs while scoring 173
   (b) Tendulkar scored 148 and got past 4000 runs in Test cricket
   (c) Srinath reached 100 wickets in Test Matches
   (d) All the above

84. At which venue did Sachin surpass the record of great Don Bradman of scoring the 29th century with his knock of 193 runs in the 3rd Test against England on 20 April 2002?
(a) Edgbaston
(b) Headingley
(c) The Oval
(d) Manchester

85. In which year did Sachin, while playing against Sri Lanka in Delhi on 10 December 2005, score his 35th ton to surpass the record of Sunil Gavaskar of most centuries in Test cricket?
(a) 2004 (b) 2005
(c) 2006 (d) 2007

86. At which venue in West Indies did Sachin complete his 8000 Test runs while scoring 86 runs in the second innings of the final match in 2002?
(a) St. John's, Antigua
(b) Bourda, Georgetown, Guyana
(c) Sabina Park, Kingston
(d) Queen's Oval, Port of Spain

87. How many batsmen had already completed their 10,000 Test runs in a course of playing against Pakistan at the Eden Gardens, Kolkata16 March 2005?
(a) One
(b) Two
(c) Three
(d) Four

88. When Sachin scored 88 runs in the first innings of the second Test at Mohali from 17- 21 October 2008 against Australia, which milestone(s) did he achieve?

I. He crossed 12000 Test runs

II. He scored his 50th half-century in Tests

III. He completed his 150 Test matches

Which combination is true?

(a) I only (b) II only

(c) I & II (d) I & III

89. Playing where did Tendulkar pass 12000 runs in ODI during his quick innings of 98 against Pakistan defeating them by six wickets on 1 March 2003 in the 2003 World Cup?

(a) Cape Town (b) Bulawayo

(c) Centurion (d) Pietermaritzburg

90. Where in 2010 did Tendulkar pass 13,000 Test runs while scoring his 44th Test century (105) in his 267th innings?

(a) Wellington (b) Ahmedabad

(c) Mirpur (d) Chittagong

91. In which innings of which Test match against Australia did Tendulkar pass the 14000 Test runs' mark during the Aussies' visit to India in 2010? It was when he scored:

(a) 98 runs in the 1st innings of the 1st Test in Mohali

(b) 38 runs in the 2nd innings of the 1st Test in Mohali

(c) 214 runs in the 1st innings of the 2nd Test in Bangalore

(d) 53 runs in the 2nd innings of the 2nd Test in Bangalore

92. While scoring his 43rd century (100*) in the first Test against Sri Lanka in Ahmedabad on 20 November 2009, he became the first person to achieve which landmark?
(a) Completing 10,000 runs in Test cricket
(b) Scoring 12000 runs in Tests
(c) Scoring 30,000 runs in international cricket
(d) Scoring a hundred against each Test playing nation

93. At which venue did Sachin surpass Brian Lara's record of most runs in Test matches (11,953) while playing in the Border-Gavaskar Trophy series on 17 October 2008?
(a) Melbourne
(b) Hobart
(c) Mohali
(d) Ahmedabad

94. Whose record of 168 Test matches did Sachin surpass in 2010 to become the most capped player in the world?
(a) Allan Border
(b) Gary Sobers
(c) Mark Waugh
(d) Steve Waugh

95. Which among the following is true about Sachin when he completed 14,000 runs in Test matches to set a new record, while in Bangalore on 10 November 2011?
(a) He hit a ton
(b) He shared the most tons scored by Gavaskar and Azharuddin in Bangalore
(c) He was playing against the Aussies
(d) All the above

96. By scoring 33 runs in his last T20 match (IPL) on 5 October 2013, Sachin set a new record of crossing 50,000 runs in 953 competitive matches. What is his final tally?
(a) 50,009 runs (b) 51,009 runs
(c) 52,009 runs (d) 53,009 runs

97. Against which country has Sachin reached another landmark, that of scoring 15,000 ODI runs on 29 June 2007 in Belfast, Ireland?
(a) Ireland (b) South Africa
(c) England (d) Kenya

98. In 2002, Sachin completed 8,000 runs and created a record of doing so in the fastest time in terms of innings (154). Whose record of doing so in 157 innings did he surpass?
(a) Jeoff Boycott (b) Colin Cowdrey
(c) Garfield Sobers (d) Greg Chappelle

99. Whose Indian record of playing most Tests (131) did Sachin surpass on 18 March 2006 in his home town?
(a) Sunil Gavaskar (b) Kapil Dev
(c) Anil Kumble (d) None of these

100. Where in South Africa did Sachin score his 50th Test hundred (111) against the hosts on 19 December 2010?
(a) Centurion (b) Cape Town
(c) Natal (d) Bloemfontein

101. How did Sachin complete the 51st and last Test century (146) of his career against South Africa on 4 January 2011? It was by hitting a:
(a) Double (b) Single
(c) Four (d) Six

102. What is the final tally of Test runs in his career of 200 matches, highest by any player in the world with an average of 53.78?
(a) 15621 (b) 15721
(c) 15821 (d) 15921

103. Sachin is the only cricketer in the world to have nearly 16,000 runs and taking more than 45 wickets in his 200 Test matches. How many Test wickets has he taken in 4240 balls that he threw conceding 2,492 runs with an economy rate of 3.52?
(a) 46 (b) 47
(c) 48 (d) 49

104. In which year was Tendulkar awarded the prestigious Arjuna Award along with Jaspal Rana (shooting), Rosa Kutty (athletics), Jude Felix (hockey), Kernam Malleswari (weightlifting), Rajendra Singh (rowing), and kabaddi players Rajarathnam and Ashok D. Shinde?
(a) 1994 (b) 1995
(c) 1996 (d) 1997

105. The most prestigious and oldest individual cricket award is *Wisden,* which selects five outstanding cricketers every year and is termed as *Wisden Cricketer of the Year.* Sachin and P. Simmons were two among these players who received this award in the year 1997. Which among the following cricketers from the Indian subcontinent did not get it that year?
(a) Saeed Anwar (b) Mushtaq Ahmed
(c) Wasim Akram (d) Sanath Jayasuriya

106. Named after the former Prime Minister of India, the *Rajeev Gandhi Khel Ratna Award* is the highest and most prestigious among the Indian awards given to most outstanding sports person every year since 1991-92. When did Tendulkar receive this award?
(a) 1996-97 (b) 1997-98
(c) 1998-99 (d) 1999-2000

107. Padma Shri is the fourth highest civilian award given by India to persons for their contribution in various spheres of activity. Sachin received this prestigious award in 1999. Who among the following sport personalities also got this award along with the Little Master in that particular year?
(a) Pargat Singh (b) Karnam Malleswari
(c) Shiny Wilson (d) Santosh Yadav

108. For which year was Sachin Tendulkar awarded *Padma Vibhushan*, India's second highest civilian award along with luminaries like Asha Bhonsle, Ratan Tata, Pranab Mukherjee, Lakshmi Niwas Mittal, Edmund Hillary, E. Shreedharan, Narayana Murty, and few others?
(a) 2004 (b) 2005
(c) 2006 (d) 2008

109. Since 2004, the International Cricket Council (ICC) gives a set of awards known as "ICC Awards" every year in order to honour the best international players of the previous twelve months in various categories. In which year did Sachin Tendulkar win the *ICC Cricketer of the Year* title, the highest official award by the ICC in the seventh ICC awards ceremony held in Bangalore?
(a) 2007 (b) 2008
(c) 2009 (d) 2010

110. In which two successive years was Sachin Tendulkar awarded the ICC World Test XI?
(a) 2007, 2008 (b) 2008, 2009
(c) 2009, 2010 (d) 2010, 2011

111. How many times has Tendulkar won the ICC World ODI XI award officially sponsored by the International Cricket Counsel?
(a) Two (b) Three
(c) Four (d) Five

112. Against which country has Sachin Tendulkar made his highest score (141) in the ICC Champions Trophy?
(a) England (b) Australia
(c) Sri Lanka (d) West Indies

113. Which media agency in August 2003 awarded Sachin Tendulkar the "Greatest Sportsman" of the country in the sports category?
(a) NDTV (b) ABP News
(c) Zee News (d) Aaj Tak

114. Which prestigious international magazine named Sachin Tendulkar as (one of the) Asian Hero in November 2006?
(a) The New Yorker (b) The Week
(c) Fortune (d) Time

115. Which Indian newspaper launched a campaign called "India Poised" to celebrate India's christening of 2007 as the 'Year of India' and nominated Sachin Tendulkar as the 'Face of New India'?
(a) The Hindu (b) Hindustan Times
(c) The Indian Express (d) The Times of India

116. Which media agency in February 2010 declared Sachin Tendulkar as the "Sports Icon of the Year" at the agency's Indian of the Year Awards?
(a) NDTV (b) BBC World
(c) ABP News (d) IBN Live

117. Tendulkar started his Test career in the year 1989. In which season was he awarded the Man of the Match title for the first time scoring 68 and 119 in the two innings besides taking two catches against England at Old Trafford, Manchester?
(a) 1990 (b) 1992-93
(c) 1994 (d) 1995

118. Which award was presented to Sachin Tendulkar in 2011 by the famous Saibaba Temple Trust at Shirdi in Maharashtra, the first person to receive this prestigious award?
(a) Sai Shree (b) Sai Vibhushan
(c) Sai Bhushan (d) Sai Ratna

119. Which award along with a trophy and a cheque of five lakh rupees was given to Sachin Tendulkar by the BCCI for the best cricketer of the year 2009-10?
(a) Spirit of Cricket Award (b) Col. C. K. Nayudu Award
(c) Test Player of the Year (d) Polly Umrigar Award

120. Name the cricket website that gave Sachin Tendulkar the *Coopers and Lybrand Award* for best Test cricketer of the Year on 23 June 1998, based on performances in that calendar year?
(a) Cricketer (b) CricBuzz
(c) CricInfo (d) cricket.123india

121. Which honorary rank was given to Sachin Tendulkar by the Indian Air Force, the first sportsperson and the first personality without an aviation background to be entitled so?
(a) Wing Commander (b) Squadron Leader
(c) Group Captain (d) Air Commodor

122. Which of the following statements is correct about Sachin Tendulkar? He is the only Indian cricketer to get
(a) Padma Shri (b) Arjuna Award
(c) Rajiv Gandhi Khel Ratna (d) All of the above

123. Which was the first official award that was bestowed on him in 1994?
(a) Wisden Cricketer of the Year
(b) LG People's Choice Award
(c) Padma Shri
(d) Sandeep Reddy Award

124. Sachin Tendulkar is the only cricketer of the current generation to be included in the playing squad by whose team:
(a) International Cricket Council World Test XI
(b) Wisden 2013 Eleven
(c) Sir Don Bradman's Eleven
(d) World Cup International XI

125. Besides Rajiv Gandhi University of Health Sciences, which other university gave Sachin Tendulkar an honorary doctorate?
(a) Mumbai University (b) Mysore University
(c) Rajasthan University (d) Chandigarh University

126. Sir Garfield Sobers Trophy is a cricket shield awarded annually by the International Cricket Council (ICC) to the world player of the year. In which year was Sachin chosen for this award?
(a) 2004 (b) 2006
(c) 2008 (d) 2010

127. Which highest civilian award under the Maharashtra State was given to Sachin Tendulkar in 2001?
(a) Maharashtra Bhushan Award
(b) Maharashtra Ratna Award
(c) Maharashtra Seva Award
(d) Maharashtra Sports Award

128. Sachin Tendulkar spoke to the media after taking the oath in Rajya Sabha, "Cricket has given me everything. I wanted to give something in return to cricket in the latter half of my life. Becoming the member of Rajya Sabha, I am in a better position to help cricket and also other sports." When was he officially honoured as the Member of Parliament in Rajya Sabha?
(a) 5 February 2012
(b) 5 April 2012
(c) 5 June 2012
(d) 5 August 2012

129. Where on 28 January 2011 was Sachin awarded for outstanding achievement in sports and the People's Choice Award at The Asian Awards ceremony?
(a) New Delhi (b) Sydney
(c) London (d) Dubai

130. When was the BCCI Cricketer of the Year award given to Sachin Tendulkar?
(a) 31 May 2010 (b) 31 May 2011
(c) 31 May 2012 (d) 31 May 2013

131. Which cricket Association honoured Sachin by renaming the Kandivili Ground as the Sachin Tendulkar Gymkhana Club on 11 November 2013, before his last Test match on the Children's Day?
(a) ICC (b) BCCI
(c) MCA (d) MCI

132. The Indian government decided to confer the Bharat Ratna to Sachin on 16 November 2013, the same day that he retired from competitive cricket. He dedicated this award to his mother. He is the youngest person to be awarded Bharat Ratna, as also the only sports person to be honoured with it. Who was the last person to get it way back in 2008?
(a) Bismillah Khan (b) Gopinath Bordoloi
(c) C.N.R Rao (d) Bhimsen Joshi

133. Which famous Australian who holds the record for the highest score (380) for the Aussies in Tests, and also plays for the Chennai Super Kings in the IPL once rightly remarked about Tendulkar, "I have seen GOD, he bats at no. 4 for India in Tests"?
(a) Justin Langer
(b) Mark Waugh
(c) *Mathew Hayden*
(d) Ricky Ponting

134. Which former Indian cricket captain, known for his six sixes in an over, and also gives commentary once said about the Little Master, "He is someone sent from up there to play cricket and go back"?
(a) Sunil Gavaskar (b) Navjot Singh Sidhu
(c) Rahul Dravid (d) Ravi Shastri

135. Which New Zealand's former Test captain, famous for devising new ideas like using the spinners to open the bowling attack, once remarked about Sachin's technique of batting, "The shot played on this ball is only possible for the GOD of cricket"?
(a) John Wright (b) Martin Crowe
(c) Daniel Vettori (d) Ken Rutherford

136. "Sachin is a genius, I am a mere mortal!" Which great West Indian player who holds the record of scoring most number of runs in a single over in a Test match remarked thus about Sachin?
(a) Vivian Richards (b) Chris Gayle
(c) Brian Lara (d) Garfield Sobers

137. Which great admirer of Sachin, whose record of the most capped Test cricketer was broken by Sachin himself, was very correct when he said, "There is no shame losing to such a great player"?
(a) Steve Waugh
(b) Adam Gilchrist
(c) Geoff Marsh
(d) Clive Lloyd

138. Though down with a number of controversies, especially trying to put an end to the career of Ganguly, which former Australian captain and later a coach of Indian team, once uttered, "He is a perfectly balanced batsman and knows perfectly well when to attack and when to play defensive cricket. He has developed the ability to treat bowlers all over the world with contempt and can destroy any attack with utmost ease"?
(a) Ian Chappell (b) Greg Chappell
(c) Bob Simpson (d) Kim Hughes

139. During a Test match in Chennai in 1997, which former Australian captain said, "We did not lose a team called India...we lost to a man called Sachin"?
(a) Mark Taylor (b) Steve Waugh
(c) Mark Waugh (d) Ian Chappell

140. "He is cool, has magnificent temperament, and is so mature you tend to forget his age. I can't think of any other example of a player who has so dominated the world before the age of twenty-five." Famous for losing the captainship because his help to Kerry Packer for initiating World Series Cricket, which England former captain said these words?
(a) Tony Lewis (b) Graham Gooch
(c) Tony Greig (d) Mike Brearley

141. Considered to be one of the founders of reverse swing bowling, which great Pakistani bowler, ranked as the best bowler in ODI of all time, and bowling coach of Kolkata Knight Riders once expressed, "Today, he showed the

world why he is considered the best batsman around. Some of the shots he played were simply amazing. Earlier, opposing teams used to feel that Sachin's dismissal meant they could win the game. Today, I feel that the Indian players, too, feel this way"?

(a) Wasim Akram (b) Waqar Younis
(c) Imran Khan (d) Shoaib Akhtar

142. Former Yorkshire captain and a solid opening batsman, which British player, famous for his commentary, testifies Sachin this way: "Technically, you can't fault Sachin. Seam or spin, fast or slow, nothing is a problem."

(a) Colin Cowdrey (b) Ray Illingworth
(c) Derek Randall (d) Geoffrey Boycott

143. "I think he is marvellous. I think he will fit in whatever category of cricket that has been played or will be played, from the first ball that has ever been bowled to the last bowl that's going to be. He can play in any era and at any level." Which great West Indian player, regarded as the greatest ODI batsmen of all time and the only great batsman to play without using a helmet, said this about Sachin?

(a) Alvin Kalicharan (b) Gordon Greenidge
(c) Brian Lara (d) Vivian Richards

144. Which bowler, one of the greatest spinners in the world and one of the five *Wisden Cricketers of the Century* always feared Tendulkar? He once expressed his views about Sachin, "I would go to bed having nightmares of Sachin dancing down the ground and hitting me for sixes"?

(a) Peter Taylor (b) Jason Gillespie
(c) Glenn McGrath (d) Shane Warne

145. Watching Sachin's batting in Sydney, which tennis legend remarked, "Sachin was so focused. He never looked like getting out. He was batting with single-minded devotion. It was truly remarkable. It was a lesson."?
(a) Lesley Hunt (b) Evonne Goolagong
(c) Margaret Smith Court (d) Martina Navratilova

146. Regarding similarity between Sachin and himself, who said the following: "I saw him playing on television and was struck by his technique, so I asked my wife to come look at him. Now I never saw myself play, but I feel that this player is playing much the same as I used to play, and she looked at him on television and said yes, there is a similarity between the two...."
(a) Sir Richard Hadlee (b) Sir Leonard "Len" Hutton
(c) Michael Colin Cowdrey (d) Sir Don Bradman

147. Century-maker in England's win over Australia when Jim Laker took 19 wickets in 1956, which church minister-turned cricketer-turned umpire who saw Tendulkar playing on the pitch once said, "Sachin Tendulkar! If he isn't the best player in the world, I want to see the best player in the world."?
(a) Darrell Hair (b) Simon Taufel
(c) Dickie Bird (d) David Shepherd

148. "There are two kinds of batsmen in the world. One Sachin Tendulkar. Two all the others," remarked a former captain of Zimbabwe, considered to be the best cricketer of his country. Name him.
(a) Grant Flower (b) Andy Flower
(c) David Houghton (d) Alistair Campbell

149. The only cricketer in history to be involved in 100 Test victories, which former Australian captain spoke about Sachin sometime back: "Sachin is the most complete batsman I have seen. His technique is so good and he has played well in all conditions. To have 41 one-day international tons shows what an appetite he has for scoring runs."
(a) Steve Waugh (b) Richie Benaud
(c) Ricky Ponting (d) Allan Border

150. "He has everything a top batsman needs. Tendulkar is a classic example of a player being so good that his age is an irrelevance." Which former Zimbabwe captain and incidentally the youngest ever Zimbabwean to make a first-class century, remarked after India won the Coca Cola Cup final at Sharjah in November 1998?
(a) Stuart Carlisle (b) Andy Flower
(c) Heath Streak (d) Alistair Campbell

151. Which former Indian cricketer, politician, TV anchor and commentator, teetotaller and vegetarian, and most famous for his witty one liners once spoke about Tendulkar, "His mind is like a computer. He stores data on bowlers and knows where they are going to pitch the ball"?
(a) Kirti Azad (b) Mohammad Azharuddin
(c) Vinod Kambli (d) Navjot Sidhu

152. Name the badminton player who put Sachin's talent thus: "Tendulkar is a legend. I respect him like God. He is inspiration to all the sportspersons in India."
(a) Jwala Gutta (b) Nikhil Kanetkar
(c) Saina Nehwal (d) Pullela Gopichand

153. Which leading Bollywood actor said on 12 November 2009 in an interview to *The Times of India*: "Sachin is a true genius and a consummate artist who is gifted in handling pressure under all circumstances. It is Sachin's ability to be patient and making 'his bat to do the talking' that helps him stay away from controversies. Everyone in my family is a huge Tendulkar fan"?
(a) Aamir Khan
(b) Shahrukh Khan
(c) Dharmendra
(d) Amitabh Bachchan

154. Which Australian Prime Minister once said: "From one cricket mad nation to another, we salute the 'Little Master'. May I say on behalf of all Australian cricket fans that if Sachin does decide it is time to retire, we would support him wholeheartedly."
(a) Kevin Michael Rudd
(b) Julia Eileen Gillard
(c) Anthony John Abbot
(d) John Winston Howard

155. Soon after Tendulkar hit the century of centuries against Bangladesh, which Union Minister sent him a message, "I join the nation in congratulating Sachin Tendulkar on his making history – a hundred centuries. He has made India proud."
(a) Ajai Maken, then Sports Minister
(b) Sharad Pawar, then Agriculture Minister
(c) Pranab Mukherjee, then Finance Minister
(d) Manmohan Singh, then Prime Minister

156. Which present or former President of the BCCI wrote after Tendulkar hit his 100th ton, "Ever since he made his international debut in November 1989, Sachin Ramesh Tendulkar has strode cricketing arenas the world over, like a colossus. He has broken old records and set new benchmarks. He has been an inspiration to billions, and an ornament to the sport. 16 March 2012 will never be forgotten by cricket-lovers."
(a) I. S. Bindra (b) Raj Singh Dungarpur
(c) Jagmohan Dalmiya (d) Narayanaswami Srinivasan

157. Which member of the ICC Executive Board expressed his feelings upon Sachin's great achievement of scoring his 100th century:
"Fans have admired Sachin for more than 20 years and have recently waited with great expectation for his 100th international century. The number 100 is special for a batsman and to record 100 centuries for your country is a massive statement. He is a marvel to cricket lovers around the world and with an array of batting records, Sachin is a true role model who will undoubtedly hold a special place in cricket history."
(a) Allan Issac (b) Walter Edwards
(c) Haroon Logat (d) Dr. Julian Hunte

158. Which Indian Test opener stated on twitter: "@sachin_rt paaji congratulations! It's a small thing for you but a phenomenal historic achievement. Dinner's on me when we meet. Many more!"
(a) Sourav Ganguly (b) Virender Sehwag
(c) Gautam Gambhir (d) Wasim Jaffer

159. Which former Indian Test player expressed on twitter: "The focus today should not be about he got his 100th hundred, but how he got his 100 hundreds."
(a) Vinod Kambli (b) Mohinder Amarnath
(c) Sanjay Manjrekar (d) Sunil Gavaskar

160. Which player was so inspired by Sachin's 100th International century by expressing:
"In fact, when he scored that 100, it was the semi-finals day. I got a lot of inspiration from him. I told myself I also have to do well. I can also win the title…that also happened. I thank him for giving me that inspiration on that day."
(a) Pankaj Advani (b) Leander Paes
(c) Saina Mirza (d) Saina Nehwal

161. A day after scoring his 100th hundred, Sachin received a bouquet, comprising 100 red roses and was cutting a cake in the relaxing mood. Who presented him these gifts?
(a) M.S. Dhoni, Captain of Indian Cricket team
(b) Narayanaswami Srinivasan, BCCI President
(c) Haroon Lorgat, ICC Chief
(d) Pankaj Saran, Indian High Commissioner in Dhaka

PART V

Miscellaneous

01. Which was the first occasion when Sachin was the victim of the nervous nineties, getting out for 96 runs bowled by Anurasiri?
    (a) Second Test against Sri Lanka at the Sinhalese Sports Club Ground, Colombo
    (b) First Test against Sri Lanka at the KD Singh Babu Stadium, Lucknow in 1994
    (c) Second Test against Sri Lanka at the M Chinnaswamy Stadium, Bangalore, 1994
    (d) Third Test against Sri Lanka at Ahmedabad

02. Trailing by 260 runs, India did well in the second knock at Trent Bridge, Nottingham, scoring 424 for the loss of 8 wickets in the second Test against England, played from 8-12 August, 2002 courtesy Dravid who scored a century (115). But two batsmen, though out in their nineties, also contributed to draw the match. Who missed the century by just one run, while Sachin was 8 short of a ton?
    (a) Sourav Ganguly (b) Wasim Jafar
    (c) Parthiv Patel (d) V.V.S. Laxman

03. Sachin had a good chance to hit his 35th ton to beat Gavaskar's record in the 1st Test against visiting Pakistani team in Mohali in March 2005, but at the nick of time Asim Kamal took his catch off Naved-ul-Hasan and he was robbed of this record. How many runs did Sachin score in this drawn match?

(a) 94 (b) 96
(c) 98 (d) 99

04. Tendulkar was looking for his 49th Test century in the 1st Test against Australia at Punjab Cricket Association Ground, Mohali from 1 to 5 October 2010, but unfortunately was bowled lbw by North on 98. Which other Indian batsman missed his century by 14 runs?

(a) Rahul Dravid (b) Suresh Raina
(c) Gautam Gambhir (d) V.V.S. Laxman

05. When Tendulkar was approaching his 27th Test century, he was stumped in his 89th Test match, by the wicketkeeper Foster off Giles, in the 3rd Test against England in Bangalore in December 2001. What was his score?

(a) 90 (b) 93
(c) 96 (d) 99

06. The first time when Sachin missed the century by 4 runs in a Test match occurred on our Republic Day in 1994 at Bangalore. Against which country was he playing?

(a) South Africa
(b) Sri Lanka
(c) Australia
(d) Bangladesh

07. Against which country did Tendulkar miss his century by just 3 runs during the Super Six elimination round in the 2003 World Cup being played in Johannesburg on 10 March 2003, defeating the opponents by 183 runs and cruising into the semi-finals?
(a) Sri Lanka (b) New Zealand
(c) Australia (d) South Africa

08. After scoring 90 runs, Sachin was ready to score his first ODI century on 27 February 1996 in his home ground Mumbai, but he was stumped by the wicket- keeper. Against which country was he playing?
(a) New Zealand (b) Pakistan
(c) West Indies (d) Australia

09. What was the mode of Sachin's dismissal when on 27th March 1997 he was short of just 8 runs in his century at the Test match against West Indies at Bridgetown?
(a) Stumped (b) Run out
(c) Caught (d) Hit wicket

10. When was the first occasion in ODI when Sachin was out at 99 while playing against South Africa at Belfast?
(a) 2006 (b) 2007
(c) 2008 (d) 2009

11. For the third time in the year 2007, Sachin missed the century by just one run in an ODI. Who was India's opponent at Mohali?
(a) New Zealand (b) Sri Lanka
(c) Zimbabwe (d) Pakistan

12. By what margin did Sachin miss a Test century while playing against South Africa at Mumbai on 24 February 2000?
(a) One run (b) Two runs
(c) Three runs (d) Four runs

13. At which venue in India was Sachin left stranded at 96* against the Sri Lankan team in an ODI on 21st December 2009?
(a) Indore (b) Mohali
(c) Cuttack (d) Ahmedabad

14. When was the last occasion in a Test match when Sachin missed the century (caught at 96) in his nineties while playing against West Indies at the Wankhede Stadium?
(a) 2012 (b) 2011
(c) 2010 (d) 2009

15. By what nearest margin did Sachin miss a Test century being lbw, against Australia at Mohali on 1 October 2010?
(a) 1 run (b) 2 runs
(c) 3 runs (d) 4 runs

16. How many times was Sachin out in nervous nineties in Test matches in his career?
(a) 8 (b) 9
(c) 10 (d) 11

17. How many times was Sachin dismissed in nervous nineties in ODI matches?
(a) 11 (b) 13
(c) 15 (d) 17

18. When was the last occasion when Sachin was a few runs short of his century in ODI and was caught at 91 against Australia at Brisbane?
    (a) 2007 (b) 2008
    (c) 2009 (d) 2010

19. The only occasion when Sachin was declared run out in any ODI or a Test match while on his way to score a century against South Africa was on 26 June 2007. What was his score that time?
    (a) 96 (b) 97
    (c) 98 (d) 99

20. How many times was Sachin declared out lbw in his nineties in Test innings?
    (a) 1 (b) 2
    (c) 3 (d) 4

21. On ten occasions, Sachin was dismissed in his 90s in Test matches. Which country had the privilege to get him out most times (4)?
    (a) England (b) Australia
    (c) Sri Lanka (d) Pakistan

22. Against which country was Sachin dismissed in his 90s for most times (5/17) in ODIs?
    (a) Sri Lanka
    (b) Pakistan
    (c) South Africa
    (d) England

23. Though India chased Pakistan's score of 273 runs and eventually won the game by six wickets on 1 March 2003 at Centurion in the 2003 World Cup, the Player of the Match Tendulkar missed his century. What was his score when he was caught by Younis Khan off Shoaib Akhtar?
(a) 99 (b) 98
(c) 97 (d) 96

24. On the tour of which country in 2007 did Sachin miss the centuries within the span of three days by scoring 99 and 93 runs, respectively in ODIs?
(a) New Zealand (b) Australia
(c) South Africa (d) West Indies

25. What was the mode of Sachin's dismissal in his League match against Australia in Mumbai when he was ten runs short of his century in just 84 balls in the 1996 Wills World Cup?
(a) Caught (b) Bowled
(c) Run out (d) Stumped

26. In the second Test in Sri Lanka–India series in 1993-94, played at the M. Chinnaswamy Stadium, Bangalore (26-30 January 1994), India crushed Sri Lanka by an innings and 95 runs. Navjot Sidhu (99) and Sachin were the victims of nervous nineties. By how many runs did Sachin miss the century?
(a) One (b) Two
(c) Three (d) Four

27. There were eleven occasions in Sachin's Test career where he scored a century, but India lost. Where did it happen for the first time on 3 February 1992?
(a) Perth (b) Auckland
(c) Bridgetown (d) Johannesburg

28. Under the captaincy of Tendulkar, India lost to South Africa by 282 runs in the second Test at Newlands, Cape Town, in January 1997. The captain's knock of 169 in the first innings could not avert the defeat. Which other batsman also scored a ton with a 6th wicket 222 runs partnership with Sachin?
(a) Mohd. Azharuddin
(b) Sourav Ganguly
(c) Rahul Dravid
(d) V.V.S. Laxman

29. In a dramatic finish, New Zealand won the second Test at Basin Reserve, Wellington on 30 December 1998 by 4 wickets. In India's first innings only, Sachin (47) and Azharuddin (103) dragged the total to 208, and the other nine batsmen contributed just 49 runs. What was Sachin's score in the second innings?
(a) 103 (b) 113
(c) 123 (d) 133

30. Out of 48 ODI centuries that Tendulkar scored, how many times did India lose the matches?
(a) Eleven (b) Thirteen
(c) Fifteen (d) Seventeen

31. Despite his century (116) in the first innings and a gritty half-century (52) in the second at the Melbourne Cricket Ground during the second Test match from 26-30 December 1999, Sachin could not save the match for India. Which Australian debutant was the main destroyer in his match figure of 7 wickets for 78 runs in India's defeat by 180 runs?
    (a) Glenn McGrath (b) G.S. Blewett
    (c) Brett Lee (d) W.D. Fleming

32. In the first Test match of the India-South Africa series played at Goodyear Park, Bloemfontein from 3-6 November 2001, Tendulkar hit a fine century (155), his 26th, but India lost the match by 9 wickets. Which among the following players <u>did not</u> score a ton?
    (a) Gibbs (b) Klusener
    (c) Virender Sehwag (d) D. Dasgupta

33. It is unimaginable that a team scoring 532 runs in the first innings, taking a lead of 59 runs over the opponent, faces defeat! This was exactly happened with India against Australia in the 2nd Test in Sydney during the 2007-08 tour. Tendulkar made an unbeaten score of 154 runs, but India lost the match by 122 runs. Who took India's last 3 wickets in 5 balls in the final innings when the match was due to be over in just 6 minutes?
    (a) Brett Lee
    (b) Michael Johnson
    (c) Michael Clarke
    (d) A. Symonds

34. South Africa crushed India by an inning and 6 runs in the 1st Test match in Nagpur in February 2010 despite Tendulkar's valiant effort (100) to save the match. Which other Indian was the only to score the next highest (39) in the second innings?
(a) S. Badrinath (b) W. Saha
(c) Zaheer Khan (d) Harbhajan Singh

35. Sachin made an unbeaten 111 runs in the second innings but India lost the first Test by an innings and 25 runs against South Africa played at Super Sport Park, Centurion from 16-20 December 2010. Who was the second highest scorer with 90 runs?
(a) Gautam Gambhir (b) M.S. Dhoni
(c) Rahul Dravid (d) Virender Sehwag

36. What was the winning margin for Pakistan in an ODI played in Rawalpindi on 16 March 2004, when India gave Pakistan a target of 330 runs, courtesy Sachin's brilliant 141 runs?
(a) 3 (b) 6
(c) 9 (d) 12

37. In one crucial Test match during the 1998-99 season in Chennai, the Master Blaster smashed 136 runs against the tourists but lost the match by just 12 runs. Who were the opponents?
(a) Zimbabwe
(b) South Africa
(c) New Zealand
(d) Pakistan

38. 16 March 2012 was the much awaited moment in the life of the Little Master when he scored his 100th century in International cricket (Tests & ODIs) by scoring 114 against Bangladesh in the Asia Cup at the Shere Bangla National Stadium, Dhaka, but India lost the match. How many balls were remaining when the hosts hit the winning stroke?
    (a) One (b) Two
    (c) Three (d) Four

39. In the nail-biting finish in the first Test in Chennai in January 1999, India required just 17 runs to take the lead over Pakistan. Tendulkar had scored 136 runs but the last three Indians added just four runs and Pakistan won the match by 12 runs. Who was the main destroyer taking 10 wickets for 187 runs in the match?
    (a) Nadeem Khan (b) Saqlain Mushtaq
    (c) Wasim Akram (d) Waqar Younis

40. The first Test match at Edgbaston, Birmingham from 6-10 June 1996 ended in little over three days where England defeated India by eight wickets in a low-scoring match. In India's second innings, Sachin made 122 out of India's total of 219. With 18 runs on the board, who was the highest run-getter after Tendulkar?
    (a) Ajay Jadeja (b) Mohd. Azharuddin
    (c) Nayan Mongia (d) Sanjay Manjrekar

41. Out of the 100 international centuries that Sachin Tendulkar had scored so far, how many of these have come in losing causes?
    (a) 24 (b) 25
    (c) 26 (d) 27

42. India was in a winning situation with 271/3 on the board in a league match of the 1996 Wills World Cup at the Feroz Shah Kotla, Delhi against Sri Lanka, but Sachin's century could not save India from losing the match by four wickets. How many runs did Sachin score in as many balls?
    (a) 107 (b) 117
    (c) 127 (d) 137

43. Where was the last instance when Sachin scored a ton (unbeaten 111 against South Africa) in 2010 but India lost the Test match?
    (a) Nagpur (b) Cape Town
    (c) Colombo (d) Gwalior

44. How many Test matches had Sachin already played when he notched up his fiftieth Test ton of his career (111) on 19 December 2010 against South Africa at the Super Sport Park, though India lost the match?
    (a) 164 (b) 170
    (c) 174 (d) 180

45. At which place in India in 2005 did Sachin score a century (123) in India's total of 315 against Pakistan to be sure to take 3-1 lead in the 6-match ODI series, but lost the match and the visitors levelled the series?
    (a) Nagpur
    (b) Mohali
    (c) Lucknow
    (d) Ahmedabad

46. In the first ODI of the 2006 series against Pakistan at Arbab Niaz Stadium, Peshawar, Sachin scored his 39th ton (100) and set a target of 329 runs to Pakistan who required 18 runs to win in three overs. What was the result?
(a) India won by one run
(b) Pakistan won by one wicket
(c) Match ended in a 'tie'
(d) Pakistan won by 7 runs on D/L Method

47. In an exciting 5th ODI of match of a series in 2009 in Hyderabad against Australia, the visitors set a target of 351 runs. India at one stage required 19 runs in 18 balls with 4 wickets in hand. Despite Sachin's 175 runs, India lost the match. What was the winning margin of Australia who now led 3-2?
(a) One run (b) Two runs
(c) Three runs (d) Four runs

48. What was the result in a World Cup match in 2011 played against England at Bangalore when India set a massive target of 339 runs for England to win; Sachin scoring 120. What was the result of this most exciting World Cup match?
(a) India won (b) England won
(c) It ended in a 'tie'
(d) Match was abandoned due to rain

49. Against which opponent on 12 March 2011 in a World Cup match played in Nagpur did India lose, despite scoring 296 runs mainly due to Sachin's contribution of 111?
(a) Sri Lanka (b) South Africa
(c) West Indies (d) New Zealand

50. Who was the first bowler to have 'clean bowled' Sachin in his first Test match in Karachi when he had scored 15 runs?
(a) Abdul Qadir (b) Imran Khan
(c) Waqar Younis (d) Naved Anjum

51. Sachin had a habit of being dismissed on 'lbw' very often. Who is the first bowler to have dismissed him in this fashion for the first time when he scored his first half-century?
(a) Naved Anjum (b) Imran Khan
(c) Saleem Jaffar (d) Shoaib Mohammad

52. Who was his partner when Sachin got run out for the first time in his Test career, in the second innings of Faisalabad Test in 1989-90 series after having scored 8 runs?
(a) Mohd. Azharuddin (b) Manoj Prabhakar
(c) Kiran More (d) Sanjay Manjrekar

53. During the first Test match against South Africa in 1992-93, which fielder threw the ball to Hudson to get Sachin run out for 11 when television replays were used for the first time to settle such decisions, and the square-leg umpire Cyril Mitchley followed the ruling?
(a) J.N. Rhodes (b) B.N. Schultz
(c) B.M. McMillan (d) M.W. Pringle

54. What was the mode of dismissal in Sachin's knock of 52, highest in India's innings of 213, at the Gandhi Stadium, Jalandhar on 20 February 1994 in the 3rd ODI where Sri Lanka defeated the host by 4 wickets in a rain interrupted match?
(a) Lbw (b) Caught
(c) Run out (d) Hit-wicket

55. What was the mode of dismissal when Sachin Tendulkar scored 137 runs in equal number of balls hitting 5 sixes against Sri Lanka in the Wills World Cup 1995/96 (Group A) match at the Feroz Shah Kotla, Delhi on 2 March 1996?
(a) Caught (b) Bowled
(c) Run out (d) Lbw

56. How was Sachin dismissed the most number of times (40) in six editions of the Indian Premier League?
(a) Caught (b) Bowled
(c) Leg before wicket (d) Run out

57. There is only one instance in Test cricket when Sachin was dismissed on first ball that he faced, against Pakistan on 16 February 1999. Who was the bowler who clean bowled him?
(a) Shahid Afridi (b) Nadeem Khan
(c) Shoiab Akhtar (d) Umar Gul

58. Which Australian bowler dismissed Sachin for most number of times (14) in international cricket, which in itself is a record?
(a) Glenn McGrath (b) Brett Lee
(c) Jason Gillespie (d) Shane Warne

59. Name the first bowler who got Sachin stumped out in Test matches in 2001-02 series when he was 10 short of his hundred playing against England at the M. Chinnaswamy Stadium in Bangalore?
(a) Ashley Giles (b) Matthew Hoggard
(c) Craig White (d) Andrew Flintoff

60. Sachin played his first ODI match against Sri Lanka on 25 April 1990 and just scored 10 runs before returning to the pavilion. How was he dismissed?
    (a) Hit-wicket (b) Run out
    (c) Clean bowled (d) Retired hurt

61. How many times has Sachin been dismissed on duck?
    (a) Five (b) Ten
    (c) Fifteen (d) Twenty

62. Sachin made his ODI debut on 18 December 1989 at the Municipal Stadium, Gujranwala and was dismissed for zero on the second ball when Wasim Akram took the catch on Waqar Younis's ball. How many runs did Sachin score in his second ODI on 1 March 1990 played against New Zealand before he was caught and bowled by Thomson?
    (a) 0 (b) 10
    (c) 20 (d) 30

63. Who said about Sachin, "I saw Sachin play some great innings, but two stand out. In the 1998 Test in Chennai, I dismissed him on fifth ball in the first innings…"
    (a) M.R. Whitney (b) C. J. McDermott
    (c) Brett Lee (d) Shane Warne

64. In his first ever over, how many runs did Sachin concede to a bowler while playing his first Test match in Karachi in 1989- 90?
    (a) 2 (b) 5
    (c) 10 (d) 13

65. Apart from being a top class batsman, Sachin Tendulkar is also a useful bowler, particularly when opposition's big partnership is in progress. How many wickets did Sachin take on his first tour to Australia in 1991-92, giving 104 runs in 36 overs, 10 of these maiden?

(a) One (b) Two
(c) Three (d) Four

66. Who was Sachin's first Test victim against Australia in the third Test at Sydney in 1992?

(a) M.G. Hughes (b) S.K. Warne
(c) D.N. Jones (d) M.C. McDermott

67. While Sachin could take three Australian wickets in the India-Australia 4-Test series in 2003-04 played in Australia, which bowler with 24 wickets in the series was the top 'destroyer'?

(a) Gellespie (b) McGill
(c) Harbhajan Singh (d) Anil Kumble

68. Though Sachin is well-known as a batsman, he has shown instances of being useful in getting a formidable partnership broken with his cunning bowling. With a decent figure of 6-2-7-2, he helped New Zealand to be restricted to 352 runs in their first innings in Wellington Test in December 1998. Which Kiwi pair did he dislodge who contributed 137 runs for the eighth wicket in the hosts' victory?

(a) Nash-Vettori (b) McMillan - Cairns
(c) Fleming - Horne (d) McMillan - Astle

69. Apart from scoring his first century against Pakistan at Chepauk in Chennai in the first Test match in January 1999, Sachin also demonstrated his bowling skill by taking three important wickets of the rival team. Name the Pakistan top batsman whom Sachin dismissed in both the innings?
    (a) Saeed Anwar
    (b) Inzamam-ul-Haq
    (c) Yousuf Youhana
    (d) Moin Khan

70. Besides V.V.S. Laxman's match-winning 281, Harbhajan Singh excelled in bowling with a match figure of 13 for 196 runs including a hat-trick. Tendulkar, despite having failed in batting, showed his prowess in bowling by claiming three important wickets for just 33 runs in 11 overs, 3 of the overs being maidens. By which mode did he dismissed all three?
    (a) Bowled
    (b) Leg before wicket
    (c) Caught
    (d) Caught behind the wicket

71. Great efforts from Indian bowlers were responsible for India's narrow win over Australia by 2 wickets in the third Test match at Chepauk, Chennai in March 2001 thereby levelling the series. Tendulkar restricted the Aussies by his economical bowling (38-1-78-0). How many wickets did Harbhajan Singh claim in the match?
    (a) Thirteen (b) Fourteen
    (c) Fifteen (d) Sixteen

72. In the second Test at the Adelaide Oval from 12-16 December 2003, India achieved a great victory over Australia by 4 wickets when the hosts, after making 556 runs in the first knock, succumbed to Indian pressure and could score only 196 in the second outing. Besides Tendulkar, who captured 2 wickets, which Indian bowler took 6 wickets for just 41 runs and opened the way for Indian victory?
    (a) Irfan Pathan (b) Ajit Agarkar
    (c) Zahir Khan (d) Aashish Nehra

73. Sachin has taken 46 Test wickets. Which among the following is not his style of bowling?
    (a) Right-arm off break (b) Fast bowling
    (c) Leg-break (d) Right-arm medium pace

74. In the historical first Test match of the series being played at Multan in March 2004 when India trounced Pakistan by an innings and 52 runs, courtesy Sehwag's 309 and Tendulkar's unbeaten 194, which Indian bowler was responsible for destroying Pakistan's innings by scalping 8 wickets, besides Tendulkar's two marvellous wickets?
    (a) L. Balaji (b) Irfan Pathan
    (c) Anil Kumble (d) Zaheer Khan

75. The third and final Test against New Zealand played in Wellington in April 2009 was destined for a draw until Sachin was given the ball by skipper Dhoni after 76 overs were already bowled in New Zealand's second innings. Sachin obliged, but rain spoiled the victory when the hosts were 8 down and still 118 runs behind. How many wickets did Sachin take to increase his tally of Test wickets to 44?
    (a) Two (b) Three
    (c) Four (d) Five

76. At times Tendulkar is handed over the ball when two batsmen on the opposite side are firmly stable and the little master plays the trick in few overs. In the 3rd Test match between India and South Africa played in Cape Town in January 2011 whose wicket did Tendulkar dismiss ending a partnership of 103 runs?
    (a) Jacques Kallis
    (b) Mark Boucher
    (c) AG Prince
    (d) D Steyn

77. More than his score of 141 runs in 128 balls, it was Sachin's bowling that won the ICC 1998 quarterfinal at Dhaka against Australia. How many wickets did Sachin take in that important match?
    (a) Two (b) Three
    (c) Four (d) Five

78. How many wickets has Sachin Tendulkar taken in his 463 ODI matches?
    (a) 124 (b) 134
    (c) 144 (d) 154

79. Australia was chasing Indian target of 310 to win and by the 30th over had scored 203 for the loss of 3 wickets in an ODI match. Suddenly Sachin turned the match in India's favour by his accurate bowling and gave just 32 runs in 10 overs. How many wickets did he take in that match?
    (a) Two (b) Three
    (c) Four (d) Five

80. Which Pakistani player's catch was Sachin's first in Test matches (on the bowling of Manoj Prabhakar)?
(a) Rameez Rana (b) Javed Miandad
(c) Wasim Akram (d) Saleem Malik

81. On whose bowling did Sachin take his first ever catch in the Champions League and got rid of J.D. Vandiar of the Kings XI Punjab on 10 September 2013 played at New Wanderers Stadium, Johannesburg?
(a) K. Polard (b) R. Mclaren
(c) S.L. Malinga (d) A.G. Murtaza

82. The 41-year old Omar Henry, the first non-white cricketer of South African team, was the second batsman caught by Sachin for 3 runs in the first Test against South Africa at Durban in 1992. Who was the bowler?
(a) Anil Kumble (b) Javagal Srinath
(c) Manoj Prabhakar (d) Ravi Shastri

83. How many catches has Sachin taken in his first Test match series of five matches in 1991- 92 tour of Australia?
(a) One (b) Two
(c) Three (d) Four

84. Who was the first player from Pakistan to become a victim of Sachin Tendulkar in any World Cup on 4 March 1992 played at SCG, Sydney in which India defeated Pakistan by 43 runs?
(a) Moin Khan (b) Inzamam-ul-Haq
(c) Aamer Suhail (d) Saleem Malik

85. It was the semi-final match of the Hero Cup against the South Africans at Eden Gardens, Kolkata on 24 November 1993. The visiting team needed just six runs to win in the ultimate over. An 'inexperienced' 20-year-old Sachin took the ball from the skipper abruptly and showed his bowling prowess, took wickets and denied the visitors a victory. Who was the bewildered skipper?
    (a) Kapil Dev (b) K. Srikkanth
    c) Mohd. Azharuddin (d) Dilip Vengsarkar

86. How many catches did Sachin take in 463 ODI matches, thus finishing at the fourth position?
    (a) 140 (b) 150
    (c) 160 (d) 170

87. Against which two countries has Sachin taken most catches (19) in his 177 Test matches?
    (a) England and Australia
    (b) Australia and South Africa
    (c) South Africa and Sri Lanka
    (d) Sri Lanka and Australia

88. Against which country did Sachin become the first Indian player to score a century and capture four wickets in the same ODI at Dhaka on 28 October 1998?
    (a) Zimbabwe (b) Bangladesh
    (c) West Indies (d) Australia

89. What was Sachin's best bowling performance in 67 ODIs matches that he played against Pakistan while taking 29 wickets?
    (a) 2 for 20 (b) 3 for 30
    (c) 4 for 40 (d) 5 for 50

90. In which year was Sachin chosen as captain of Indian cricket team?
    (a) 1995 (b) 1996
    (c) 1997 (d) 1998

91. How old was Sachin when he became skipper of Indian cricket team?
    (a) 21 (b) 22
    (c) 23 (d) 24

92. Whom did Sachin replace as a captain on 29 July 1999 for his second stint as a captain?
    (a) Rahul Dravid (b) Mohd. Azharuddin
    (c) Virender Sehwag (d) Sourav Ganguly

93. When his captain could not continue the play due to fever, Sachin deputised the Indian squad against Sri Lanka in the 3rd Test of 5-Test series (4-9 August 1993) being played at the Saravanamuttu Stadium, Colombo. Who was the captain he deputised?
    (a) Kapil Dev (b) Mohd. Azharuddin
    (c) Navjot Sidhhu (d) Manoj Prabhakar

94. In how many Test matches did Sachin lead the Indian side after he took over as captain in 1996?
    (a) 15 (b) 20
    (c) 25 (d) 30

95. Sachin's tenures as captain were not very successful, which is why he voluntarily resigned from the post. How many times (out of 25) did India win Test matches under Sachin's captaincy?
    (a) 4 (b) 5
    (c) 6 (d) 7

96. In the 73 ODIs that Sachin played as the captain of the Indian cricket team, he won 23 times and lost 43 times. How many ended in a 'tie'?
   (a) None (b) One
   (c) Two (d) Three

97. During India's England tour in 2007, Sachin was appointed vice-captain to Captain Rahul Dravid who was reluctant for this tedious job. Whose name did Sachin recommend when the then BCCI President Sharad Pawar personally offered the captaincy to the Master Blaster?
   (a) Virender Sehwag
   (b) M.S. Dhoni
   (c) Anil Kumble
   (d) Sourav Ganguly

98. How many ODI centuries had Sachin scored under his own captaincy?
   (a) 4 (b) 6
   (c) 8 (d) 10

99. In an ODI against Sri Lanka at the R Premadasa Stadium, Colombo on 17 August 1997, the hosts scored 302 runs for 4 wickets in 50 overs. In the run chase, two Indians scored centuries but lost the match by 2 runs. Who were the two Indian batsmen who scored the tons?
   (a) Sachin Tendulkar and Rahul Dravid
   (b) Rahul Dravid and Sourav Ganguly
   (c) Sourav Ganguly and Mohd. Azaharuddin
   (d) Mohd. Azaharuddin and Ajay Jadeja

100. Which of the following options is <u>not true</u> as far as India under the second tenure of Sachin's captaincy?
   (a) India toured Australia in 1999 in a 3-Test series
   (b) Australia thrashed India 3-0
   (c) Sachin was adjudged the Man of the Series Award
   (d) None of these

101. On which occasion did Sachin Tendulkar lead the Indian team for the first time after the then captain Mohd. Azharuddin fell sick during India's tour of Sri Lanka in the summer of 1993?
   (a) In the first Test at Kandy which was incomplete due to rain
   (b) In the second Test where Sachin struck his first century against Sri Lanka
   (c) During the third Test in Colombo in July 2003
   (d) He never deputised in Sri Lanka

102. How was the performance of India against South Africa under Sachin's leadership in this home series of two matches in 2000?
   (a) South Africa defeated India 1-0
   (b) South Africa defeated India 2-0
   (c) India defeated South Africa 1-0
   (d) The series was levelled 1-1

103. When Sachin was captaining in the 1996-97 series in South Africa where the hosts won by 282 runs, India was reeling at 58/5 at one stage in the first innings despite Sachin's heroic 169 runs and his partnership of 222 with another centurion (115). Who was his partner in that stand?
   (a) Rahul Dravid (b) Mohd. Azharuddin
   (c) V.V.S. Laxman (d) S.S. Das

104. Tendulkar holds the current record (217 against NZ in 1999-2000) for the highest score in Test cricket by an Indian when captaining the side. With 205 runs in his kitty, which Indian captain was holding the record earlier?
(a) Mansoor Ali Khan Pataudi
(b) Ravi Shastri
(c) Gundappa Viswanath
(d) Sunil Gavaskar

105. "When Sachin became captain for the first time in 1996, he was very demanding. We could not emulate him. He used to prepare for three hours for a game. He wanted to win every game and went into a shell when the team lost." Which former Indian bowler issued this statement?
(a) Anil Kumble (b) Ajit Agarkar
(c) Javagal Srinath (d) Venkatesh Prasad

106. The first Test at Durban in December 1996 was a low-score match when the total score of both the teams was 660 runs, but still South Africa defeated India by a whopping 328 runs in three days. Tendulkar, the captain, made just 15 and 4 runs in two innings. Who, with unbeaten 27, was the highest scorer in the Indian team in both innings?
(a) Sourav Ganguly (b) Rahul Dravid
(c) Anil Kumble (d) Nayan Mongia

107. Where in India did Sachin complete 1000 runs as a captain during the Indian tour of Sri Lanka in 1997-98?
(a) Mohali (b) Nagpur
(c) Mumbai (d) Kolkata

108. During the two-Test series against Bangladesh in early 2007, Sachin was appointed vice-captain of the Indian team. Who was the Indian captain?
(a) Rahul Dravid (b) Sourav Ganguly
(c) Virender Sehwag (d) M.S. Dhoni

109. In which season did Sachin lift the Ranji Trophy for the first time as a captain?
(a) 1994-95 (b) 1999-2000
(c) 2008-09 (d) 2012-13

110. In which season of the Indian Premier League (IPL) was Sachin chosen as the captain of Mumbai Indians?
(a) I; 2008-09 (b) II; 2010
(c) III; 2011 (d) IV; 2012

111. In which season of the Indian Premier League (IPL) had Sachin relinquished the role of captain of Mumbai Indians?
(a) 2010 (b) 2011
(c) 2012 (d) 2013

112. Which 'prize' did Sachin win for scoring most runs (618) in the IPL 2011 season while he was captaining the Mumbai Indians?
(a) Green Cap (b) Red Cap
(c) Orange Cap (d) Golden Cap

113. Who replaced Sachin after he stepped down as captain of Mumbai Indians ahead of the 2012 IPL session?
(a) Rohit Sharma (b) Harbhajan Singh
(c) Herschelle Gibbs (d) Kieron Pollard

114. According to Sachin Tendulkar, who are his cricket heroes?

I. Sunil Gavaskar and Chris Lloyd
II. Sunil Gavaskar, Viv Richards and Imran Khan
III. Polly Umrigar and Ajit Wadekar
IV. Sunil Gavaskar, Viv Richards, Imran Khan and Sandeep Patil

(a) I only (b) II only
(c) III only (d) IV only

115. Which is Sachin's favourite cricket ground?
(a) Wankhede Stadium (b) V. C. A. Nagpur
(c) Sydney Cricket Ground (d) Old Trafford, Manchester

116. Other than cricket, which sport does Sachin love?
(a) Tennis (b) Football
(c) Golf (d) Billiards

117. Which are Sachin's favourite non-cricketing sporting stars?
(a) Steffi Graf and Pele (b) McEnroe and Maradonna
(c) Ronaldo and Sabatini (d) Mark Spitz and Karpov

118. Which is Tendulkar's favourite magazine?
(a) Filmfare (b) Newsweek
(c) Sportstar (d) India Today

119. Sachin loves listening to music. What type of music does he like the most?
(a) Pop music (b) Classical
(c) Ghazals (d) Bollywood songs

120. Who is Sachin's favourite actress?
   (a) Kareena Kapoor
   (b) Waheeda Rehman
   (c) Shabana Azmi
   (d) Madhuri Dixit

121. Other than Amitabh Bachchan, who is Sachin's favourite actor?
   (a) Aamir Khan (b) Jackie Shroff
   (c) Nana Patekar (d) Govinda

122. Which brand of car does Sachin like the most?
   (a) Maruti (b) Rolls-Royce
   (c) Mercedes (d) Volkswagen

123. Which does Sachin enjoy eating the most?
   (a) Steak (b) Chinese
   (c) Mughlai (d) South Indian

124. Which among the following Japanese dishes are in Sachin's list of favourites?
   (a) Sushi (b) Wasabi
   (c) Tempura (d) All the above

125. When it comes to drinking, what is Sachin's favourite?
   (a) Alcohol (b) Soft drinks
   (c) Coconut water (d) Cold water

126. Which shot does Sachin enjoy playing the most?
   (a) Straight drive (b) Late cut
   (c) Hook (d) Square drive

127. When it comes to food, Sachin enjoys street food just as much. Which one is his favourite?
(a) Bakarwadi (b) Batata bhaji
(c) Vada-pao (d) Pav bhaji

128. Though Sachin is a very religious person and visits a number of temples regularly, yet which spiritual saint does he revere the most?
(a) Swami Vivekanand (b) Swami Sarvalokananda
(c) Neem Karoli' Baba (d) Shirdi Sai Baba

129. Which is Sachin's most favourite Bollywood film song sung by Lata Mangeshkar for Madan Mohan that was composed in 1966?
(a) *Mera saya sath hoga*
(b) *Lag ja gale ke phir yeh haseen raat ho na ho*
(c) *Aap ki nazron ne samjha*
(d) *Nainon mein badra chhaye*

130. The funniest moment in Sachin's cricketing days was when an Indian batsman came to the crease in 1990 at Old Trafford with a new bat and the bat was broken into two pieces on the first ball that he faced off Cris Lewis. Who was that batsman?
(a) Sanjeev Sharma (b) Narendra Hirwani
(c) Kiran More (d) Manoj Prabhakar

131. Which was the first advertisement in which Sachin was featured?
(a) Boost (b) Sticking plaster
(c) Coca Cola (d) Maggi

132. Sachin is the richest cricketer in the world by way of advertisements. Which was the first ever brand that he endorsed in 1990?
(a) Pepsi (b) Sunfeast
(c) Britannia (d) Boost

133. In which year did Sachin Tendulkar sign for Pepsi?
(a) 1991 (b) 1992
(c) 1994 (d) 1996

134. In 1995, which company related to telecommunications sector did Sachin Tendulkar sign for five-year commercial endorsements and marketing deal that made him the richest cricketer in the world?
(a) Bharti Airtel (b) Reliance Communications
(c) WorldTel (d) Siemens Communications

135. For which company who manufactures the optical products including cameras did Sachin Tendulkar sign in 2004 for a five-year contract?
(a) Canon (b) Nikon
(c) Olympus (d) Panasonic

136. With which shoe manufacturing company did Sachin sign a contract for five years in 1995?
(a) Nike (b) Reebok
(c) Lancer (d) Action

137. In which year did the ten-year contract between Adidas and Sachin Tendulkar end?
(a) 2004 (b) 2006
(c) 2008 (d) 2010

138. With which famous brand that manufactures biscuits and related food products did Sachin sign a contract in 2001 for six years?
(a) Parle (b) Sunfeast
(c) Britannia (d) Supreme Bakery

139. Which sports channel signed a contract with Sachin Tendulkar in 2002 which still continues?
(a) Star Cricket (b) ESPN Star Sports
(c) Ten Cricket (d) Neo Sports

140. Which among the following products is not in the list of Sachin's endorsements?
(a) Hero Honda (b) VISA
(c) MRF (d) Reynolds

141. Through which Mumbai-based NGO does Sachin Tendulkar sponsor 200 underprivileged children every year in association with Annabel Mehta, his mother-in-law?
(a) Bal Prafulta
(b) Aamcha Ghar
(c) Apnalaya
(d) Slum Rehabilitation Society

142. For which soft drink was Sachin enrolled in a catchy consumer one-liner TV commercial 'Oye Bubbly' created by Mind Share Ventures Group in 2005?
(a) Sprite (b) Frooti
(c) Coco Cola (d) Pepsi Co

143. For which among the following campaigns is Sachin Tendulkar <u>not</u> a spokesperson?
   (a) Luminous India
   (b) Idea
   (c) AIDS Awareness
   (d) National Egg Coordination Committee

144. Which company founded in 2006 is publishing a series of comic books featuring Sachin Tendulkar as a super hero?
   (a) Virgin Comics (b) Diamond Comics
   (c) Phantomville (d) Indrajal Comics

145. Which popular range of writing instruments manufactured by the G M Pens International roped in Sachin Tendulkar as brand ambassador by signing a 'three-year inning' with him?
   (a) Luxor (b) Parker
   (c) Reynolds (d) None of the above

146. In the Forbes list, how much money has Sachin earned from endorsements as on June 2013?
   (a) 8 million (b) 18 million
   (c) 28 million (d) 38 million

147. Which brand, named after the Little Master, was launched in Mumbai on 23 March 2010 by Santosh Desai, MD & CEO, Future Group?
   (a) SACH Toothpaste
   (b) SACH Cream
   (c) SACH Moisturiser
   (d) SACH Mouthwash

148. In which year did Sachin sign a contract with Saatchi and Saatchi's ICONIX values at 180 crore (US$33 million) for three years?
(a) 2000 (b) 2003
(c) 2006 (d) 2009

149. In Colaba, Mumbai, there is a famous joint called *Tendulkar's*. It is a:
(a) Bookshop (b) Restaurant
(c) Hotel (d) Clinic

150. Name the restaurant that Sachin has opened in Mulund, Mumbai?
(a) Sach's (b) Sachi's
(c) Sachin's (d) SRT's

151. In association with which businessman – who runs Mars Restaurants – has Sachin opened three restaurants, two in Mumbai and one in Bangalore?
(a) Santosh Desai
(b) Sanjay Narang
(c) Avinash Bhosale
(d) Sadanand Shetty

152. In 2007, Sachin announced a joint venture with the Future Group and Manipal Group under the brand name '*S Drive and Sach*'. What sort of product is it?
(a) Mercedes Car
(b) Skincare and Beauty
(c) Health and Safety
(d) Healthcare and Sports Fitness

153. Which Mangalore-based bank marketed the Tendulkar gold coins in 1999?
(a) Central Bank
(b) Punjab National Bank
(c) Corporation Bank
(d) Bank of Baroda

154. Which among the following is the oldest product that featured Sachin Tendulkar?
(a) Fiat Palio
(b) Reynolds
(c) Castrol India
(d) Coca-Cola

155. Sachin Tendulkar is the Brand Ambassador of which power company, launched on 25 September 2012 in Gurgaon that sells solar products like inverters, lanterns, home lamps, etc?
(a) Topsun Energy Ltd.
(b) Luminous India
(c) Tata Power Solar
(d) Tata BP *Solar India* Ltd

156. What is so special about Sachin's 239 matches (54 Tests and 185 ODIs) played for India in eight years between 25 April 1990 and 24 April 1998?
(a) He got a chance to lead India only after that
(b) He struck 28 centuries in this period
(c) He equalled Bradman's record of 29 centuries
(d) He did not miss a game for India in Tests or ODIs, a world record

157. In order to mark 150 years of the Wisden Cricketers' Almanac, Sachin Tendulkar is named in Wisden all-time World Test XI, announced on 24 October 2013. Which among the following facts is incorrect?
(a) Sachin's position is his favourite spot number four
(b) Sachin and Wasim Akram are the only Asians included in the team
(c) Only two of his contemporaries, Shane Warne and Akram are there
(d) None of these

158. The Little Master's feat of scoring his record double ton in ODIs against South Africa in February 2010 was included in *Time* magazine's top 10 sports moments of the year. At which venue in India did he attain this memorable record?
(a) Mohali (b) Gwalior
(c) Lucknow (d) Nagpur

159. What was the result of a Test match played in March 2004 at Multan against Pakistan in which Sachin was short of only six runs from a double century, but surprisingly the captain Rahul Dravid declared the second innings, a decision which was much criticized all over?
(a) India won the match (b) India lost the match
(c) It was a drawn match (d) It ended in a 'tie'

160. When Sachin scored 148 against Australia at Sydney in 1992, which great bowler made the debut in the game?
(a) G. McGrath (b) Michel Johnson
(c) Craig McDermott (d) Shane Warne

161. On which occasion had British artist Sacha Jafri's canvas of Sachin fetched $ 750,000 in an exhibition at Art Dubai and the money was donated to the M.S. Dhoni Foundation that provides food, water and shelter to some of the poorest children?
(a) After playing his 100th international ODI
(b) After playing his 100th international Test match
(c) After scoring his 100th international hundred
(d) After hitting two consecutive tons (143; 134) against Australia in April 1998

162. In whole of his Test career Sachin has never played/batted at which position?
(a) Opening No. 2
(b) 3: one-down
(c) 4: two-down
(d) 7: six-down

163. Which among the following facts is not true as far has Sachin is concerned in his first ever epic Ranji final for Mumbai against Haryana in 1991?
(a) He scored 47 and 96 runs in the two innings
(b) He shared a stand of 134 for the fourth wicket with Dilip Vengsarkar in the second innings
(c) Haryana won by 2 runs
(d) None of the above

164. At which Indian jail has there been a ward named after Sachin Tendulkar?
(a) Central Prison, Kannur
(b) New Delhi's Tihar Jail
(c) Yerwada Central Jail, Pune
(d) Arthur Road Jail, Mumbai

165. After hitting a couple of sixes on the bowling of inexperienced Mushtak Ahmed in an exhibition match against Pakistan at Peshawar in 1989, an experienced Abdul Qadir challenged Sachin, "*Chotu, tu ne usko to maara, meri bowling pe bhi maar.*" (You hit on his balls, now try against me too). How many consecutive sixes in one over did Sachin hit as a response?
(a) Three (b) Four
(c) Five (d) Six

166. As a cricketer, Sachin has played under six captains. Whom did he rate as the best one?
(a) Mohd. Azharuddin (b) Saurav Ganguly
(c) Rahul Dravid (d) M.S. Dhoni

167. Under the captaincy of which Indian has Sachin played the least ODIs (just 1)?
(a) Sourav Ganguly (b) Mohd. Azharuddin
(c) K. Srikkanth (d) All the above

168. Who was the captain under whom Sachin scored maximum centuries in ODIs (18)?
(a) Mohd. Azharuddin (b) M.S. Dhoni
(c) Sourav Ganguly (d) Rahul Dravid

169. During the first Test match against Sri Lanka in Chennai in December 2005, which Indian player made the debut when Tendulkar was playing his 199th Test innings?
(a) Mohd. Kaif (b) Yuvraj Singh
(c) Suresh Raina (d) M.S. Dhoni

170. What does the number 1734+ represents for Tendulkar in Test matches?
(a) Most runs scored in one calendar year
(b) Runs given as a bowler in 188 Test matches
(c) Most sixes in Test matches
(d) Most fours in Test matches

171. Which Australian cricketer accompanied Sachin on 27 August 1998 to meet the legendary Sir Donald Bradman in Adelaide on the occasion of the Australian batsman's 90th birthday celebration and remarked that Tendulkar was the best batsman in the world?
(a) Ricky Ponting (b) Ian Chappell
(c) Brett Lee (d) Shane Warne

172. In his 292 First Class matches that Sachin was asked to bowl, how many wickets has he taken with an average of 61.50?
(a) 50 (b) 60
(c) 70 (d) 80

173. During the CB series in 2008 involving India, Sri Lanka and Australia, whose tally of 11,953 runs did Sachin surpass to become the highest run-scorer in Test cricket?
(a) Sunil Gavaskar (b) Brian Lara
(c) Ricky Ponting (d) Alan Border

174. Though Sachin played his last Test match at Mumbai, where has he achieved the best average (88.18) playing 10 matches and scoring 970 runs – the most at an Indian venue?
(a) VCAG, Nagpur (b) Feroz Shah Kotla, Delhi
(c) Chepauk, Chennai (d) Chinnaswamy, Bangalore

175. Sachin has scored 21,999 runs in 538 innings of 551 List 'A' matches with an average of 45.54 and is placed third behind two players? Name them.
    (a) IVA Richards and GA Hicks
    (b) GA Hicks and GA Gooch
    (c) GA Gooch and IVA Richards
    (d) None of the above

176. Name the title of the book about Sachin written by his elder brother Ajit Tendulkar?
    (a) Sachin: Cricketer of the Century
    (b) Sachin Tendulkar: A Definitive Biography
    (c) Sachin: A Hundred Hundreds Now
    (d) The Making of a Cricketer

177. How was Sachin's performance in this tour of Australia 1999-2000?
    (a) He performed very poorly
    (b) In two matches he won the Player of the Match title
    (c) He scored three consecutive centuries
    (d) He was the Player of the Tournament, as also the Player of the Match in one of the matches

178. Sachin calls Sourav Ganguly '*Babu Moshai*'. How does Ganguly refer to him?
    (a) Chhota Babu
    (b) Little Master
    (c) Notty Boy
    (d) Sachchu

179. In his first ever tour abroad in 1989, Abdul Qadir of Pakistan at that time had some words exchanged with Sachin. Sachin replied to him by smashing him all over the field in Qadir's next over. How many runs did Sachin score in that over?
(a) 20 (6, 6, 4, 2, 2, 0 and 0 (b) 24 (6, 0, 4, 6, 6, 0 and 2)
(c) 26 (6, 6, 4, 2, 2 and 6) (d) 28 (6, 0, 4, 6, 6 and 6)

180. Name the regular Indian opening batsman who got injured in a match and Sachin was asked to open the innings on 27 March 1994 in which he scored 82 and helped India to a comfortable win over New Zealand?
(a) Kapil Dev (b) Mohd. Azharuddin
(c) Ajay Jadeja (d) Navjot Sidhu

181. Who was the commentator when Sachin scored his 35th Test century on 22 November 2005 at the Feroz Shah Kotla, Delhi?
(a) Sunil Gavaskar (b) Ravi Shastri
(c) Navjot Sidhu (d) Harsha Bhogle

182. "Can I have a drink also?" Sachin had said to an East Zone twelfth man who was serving drinks on the field during the Duleep Trophy match in Pune in 2001-02 season in which Sachin scored 199 runs. Who was this 'shy' boy who met Sachin for the first time, but failed to speak any word out of hesitation?
(a) M.S. Dhoni
(b) Wriddhiman Saha
(c) Suresh Raina
(d) Virat Kohli

183. In which Bollywood film in 2003 did Sachin make a special appearance?
(a) Rules (b) Clean Bowled
(c) Stumped (d) None of the above

184. Sachin Tendulkar became the first Indian sportsperson to grace the world-famous Madame Tussauds wax museum. Among the following famous cricketers, who else is featured here?
(a) Chris Gayle and Brian Lara
(b) Brian Lara and Shane Warne
(c) Shane Warne and Ian Chappell
(d) Ian Chappell and Brett Lee

185. Critics say Virat Kohli will overtake Sachin in many records. How old was he when Sachin faced his very first ball in 1989 against Pakistan?
(a) He was not born (b) 6 months
(c) 9 months (d) 1 year

186. Against which team at Chennai in 2013 did Sachin hit two sixes off first two balls, the only player to do so in Test cricket?
(a) Australia (b) South Africa
(c) Sri Lanka (d) New Zealand

187. In the five editions of the Indian Premier League, Sachin stands third overall with an aggregate of 2036 runs. Who tops the list with an aggregate of 2154 runs?
(a) Gautam Gambhir (b) Suresh Raina
(c) Rohit Sharma (d) Jacques Kallis

188. Which among the following was not in an exclusive club of batsmen who has not scored Test centuries against all the Test-playing nations till the time Sachin scored an unbeaten 248 against Bangladesh in Dacca in December 2004?
(a) Gary Kirsten (b) Brian Lara
(c) Steve Waugh (d) Sachin Tendulkar

189. Against which Test-playing country does Sachin have the lowest Test average (42.28)?
(a) England (b) South Africa
(c) Pakistan (d) West Indies

190. Out of 30 different cricket grounds that Sachin played in, how many centuries were scored in venues outside India?
(a) 7 (b) 14
(c) 21 (d) 27

191. At which particular moment was a special gold coin with Sachin Tendulkar's photo used when the Master Blaster walked out to play his 200th and final Test match at the Wankhede Stadium on 14 November 2013 to commemorate Tendulkar's farewell match?
(a) During toss
(b) At the Tilak ceremony with Rahul Gandhi
(c) While entering the ground
(d) At the time of his guard of honour

192. Who gave the guard of honour for Sachin's farewell Test at his home ground when Sachin walked out to play on 14 November 2013?
(a) Military band (b) Blue Frog
(c) West Indies squad (d) Bollywood stars

193. Which Indian bowler who took 5 wickets giving 40 runs against West Indies during the first innings (182 all out) in Sachin's last Test match at the Wankhede Stadium in November 2013 dedicate his wickets to "Sachin Pa-ji"?
(a) Mohammad Shami
(b) Ramchandran Ashwin
(c) Pragyan Ojha
(d) Bhuvneshwar Kumar

194. What is common among the following bowlers: Hansie Cronje, Jacob Oram, Monty Panesar, Camron White and Ujesh Ranchod? Each of them
(a) Played in IPL under Sachin's captaincy
(b) Hit for a six by Sachin on his first ball
(c) Has been a debutant wicket of Sachin
(d) Was hit for a six when Sachin was in his 90s to get his century

195. Which West Indian fielder took a sharp catch on the bowling of Narsingh Deonarayan to get Sachin out just after the first drink interval for 74 runs on 15 November 2013?
(a) Darren Sammy (b) Marlon Samuels
(c) Denesh Ramdin (d) Shivnarine Chanderpaul

196. In which year on 29 July did Sachin Tendulkar become first cricketer to play 100 overseas Test matches during the match against England at Trent Bridge?
(a) 2008 (b) 2009
(c) 2010 (d) 2011

197. Sachin has taken 102 catches in his 200 Test matches. Against which Test-playing nation has he failed to get any catch?
(a) Bangladesh (b) Zimbabwe
(c) Kenya (d) None of the above

198. How many fours did Sachin strike in 118 balls scoring 74 runs in his last Test innings played at the Wankhede Stadium in November 2013?
(a) 11 (b) 12
(c) 13 (d) 14

199. Name the new dream home that Sachin purchased in 2010 from its owners, the Satra Group, for around Rs 35 crore spread over 9000 sq feet?
(a) Sahitya Sahawas in Bandra East
(b) La Mer building in Bandra West
(c) Dorab Villa in Bandra
(d) Lokhandwala Minerva, South Mumbai

200. During the course of his first tour to Pakistan, whose bouncer left Sachin with a bleeding nose on 15 November 1989 in the last test in Sialkot?
(a) Imran Khan (b) Waqar Younis
(c) Shoaib Akhtar (d) Inzamam-ul-Haq

201. During the course of scoring 136 runs against Pakistan in Chennai in 1999, Sachin suffered severe back pain for which he discontinued playing for some time. Which country did Sachin visit for treatment?
(a) England (b) South Africa
(c) Australia (d) USA

202. Which away tour did Sachin skip in 2006 due to his shoulder injury?
(a) South Africa (b) West Indies
(c) England (d) Sri Lanka

203. Sachin played five matches for Lashing World XI to recover fitness and he remained the top scorer in all. How many tons did Sachin hit in these five games?
(a) Five (b) Four
(c) Three (d) Two

204. The visiting South African team played a three-Test series in India in 2008. During the first Test match Sachin sustained a groin injury and he missed the next two Tests. How many runs did Sachin score in the only innings that he played in the first Test?
(a) Zero (b) One
(c) Two (d) Four

205. In May 2006 Sachin missed the tour of the Caribbean for the Test series. But he agreed to play 5 games for Lashings World XI in order to regain fitness. His total score in five innings was a whopping 605 runs. Out of four centuries that he made, how many times was he retired hurt?
(a) Once (b) Twice
(c) Thrice (d) None

206. Out of 78 matches that Sachin played for Mumbai Indians in six editions of the Indian Premier League, how many times was he retired hurt?
(a) Never (b) Once
(c) Twice (d) Thrice

ANSWER KEY

Part I

Personal Life and Early Phase

1 (c), 2 (b), 3 (d), 4 (c), 5 (d), 6 (d), 7 (d), 8 (c), 9 (a), 10 (d), 11 (d), 12 (b), 13 (d), 14 (c), 15 (d), 16 (c), 17 (b), 18 (d), 19 (d), 20 (d), 21 (b), 22 (b), 23 (d), 24 (d), 25 (a), 26 (c), 27 (c), 28 (d), 29 (c), 30 (a), 31 (d), 32 (c), 33 (d), 34 (b), 35 (c), 36 (c), 37 (c), 38 (c), 39 (c), 40 (b), 41 (c), 42 (a), 43 (d), 44 (a), 45 (d), 46 (a), 47 (d), 48 (c), 49 (b), 50 (a).

51 (c), 52 (c), 53 (d), 54 (b), 55 (a), 56 (a), 57 (c), 58 (a), 59 (a), 60 (c), 61 (b), 62 (b); 63 (c), 64 (b), 65 (c), 66 (c), 67 (c), 68 (a), 69 (b), 70 (d), 71 (a), 72 (a), 73 (c), 74 (b), 75 (c), 76 (b), 77 (b), 78 (a), 79 (b), 80 (c), 81 (d), 82 (b), 83 (a), 84 (a), 85 (b), 86 (c).

Part II

Sachin's Test Career

1 (b), 2 (d), 3 (c), 4 (c), 5 (d), 6 (d), 7 (d), 8 (d), 9 (d), 10 (c), 11 (d), 12 (b), 13 (d), 14 (d), 15 (b), 16 (b), 17 (d), 18 (d), 19 (c), 20 (d), 21 (c), 22 (d), 23 (b), 24 (a), 25 (c), 26 (c), 27 (d), 28 (c), 29 (c), 30 (c), 31 (b), 32 (a), 33 (c), 34 (b),

35 (a), 36 (c), 37 (c), 38 (b), 39 (c), 40 (d), 41 (a), 42 (c), 43 (b), 44 (d), 45 (b), 46 (b), 47 (d), 48 (b), 49 (d), 50 (d).

51 (c), 52 (c), 53 (b), 54 (d), 55 (c), 56 (d), 57 (b), 58 (c), 59 (a), 60 (b), 61 (c), 62 (d), 63 (c), 64 (b), 65 (c), 66 (a), 67 (d), 68 (a), 69 (d), 70 (c), 71 (a), 72 (c), 73 (c), 74 (c), 75 (a), 76 (b), 77 (c), 78 (a), 79 (b), 80 (b), 81 (c), 82 (a), 83 (d), 84 (c), 85 (a), 86 (d), 87 (b), 88 (c), 89 (b), 90 (d), 91 (a), 92 (b), 93 (b).

Part III

Sachin in ODIs, IPL, T20 and ICC World Cup

1 (d), 2 (a), 3 (b), 4 (b), 5 (b), 6 (d), 7 (d), 8 (c), 9 (b), 10 (b), 11 (a), 12 (a), 13 (a), 14 (b), 15 (c), 16 (b), 17 (b), 18 (d), 19 (c), 20 (c), 21 (d), 22 (d), 23 (b), 24 (b), 25 (c), 26 (c), 27 (b), 28 (d), 29 (d), 30 (b), 31 (d), 32 (a), 33 (b), 34 (d), 35 (d), 36 (c), 37 (c), 38 (d), 39 (d), 40 (a), 41 (a), 42 (c), 43 (b), 44 (d), 45 (a), 46 (c), 47 (b), 48 (a), 49 (c), 50 (d).

51 (b), 52 (b), 53 (c), 54 (a), 55 (d), 56 (d), 57 (d), 58 (c), 59 (b), 60 (b), 61 (c), 62 (a), 63 (d), 64 (d), 65 (c), 66 (c), 67 (c), 68 (c), 69 (c), 70 (b), 71 (b), 72 (c), 73 (a), 74 (b), 75 (b), 76 (a), 77 (d), 78 (c), 79 (c), 80 (b), 81 (a), 82 (a), 83 (b), 84 (c), 85 (c), 86 (a), 87 (c), 88 (d), 89 (b), 90 (c), 91 (d), 92 (d), 93 (d), 94 (a), 95 (d), 96 (a), 97 (c), 98 (c), 99 (a), 100 (d). 101 (b), 102 (a), 103 (d), 104 (c).

Part IV

Awards, Accolades, Praise and Records

1 (d), 2 (d), 3 (a), 4 (b), 5 (a), 6 (c), 7 (b), 8 (d), 9 (c), 10 (b), 11 (c), 12 (a), 13 (c), 14 (a), 15 (d), 16 (b), 17 (b), 18 (d),

19 (a), 20 (b), 21 (b), 22 (d), 23 (b), 24 (b), 25 (b), 26 (c), 27 (a), 28 (c), 29 (d), 30 (a), 31 (c), 32 (d), 33 (d), 34 (d), 35 (b), 36 (b), 37 (b), 38 (a), 39 (b), 40 (c), 41 (c), 42 (d), 43 (a), 44 (d), 45 (d), 46 (d), 47 (a), 48 (c), 49 (a), 50 (a).

51 (c), 52 (a), 53 (b), 54 (b), 55 (d), 56 (b), 57 (b), 58 (d), 59 (b), 60 (d), 61 (b), 62 (a), 63 (c), 64 (d), 65 (c), 66 (d), 67 (c), 68 (a), 69 (a), 70 (c), 71 (b), 72 (d), 73 (c), 74 (c), 75 (b), 76 (b), 77 (c), 78 (c), 79 (a), 80 (c), 81 (d), 82 (d), 83 (d), 84 (b), 85 (b), 86 (c), 87 (d), 88 (c), 89 (c), 90 (d), 91 (a), 92 (c), 93 (c), 94 (d), 95 (d), 96 (a), 97 (b), 98 (c), 99 (b), 100 (a).

101 (d), 102 (d), 103 (a), 104 (a), 105 (c), 106 (b), 107 (b), 108 (d), 109 (d), 110 (c), 111 (c), 112 (b), 113 (c), 114 (d), 115 (d), 116 (a), 117 (a), 118 (d), 119 (d), 120 (c), 121 (c), 122 (d), 123 (d), 124 (c), 125 (b), 126 (d), 127 (a), 128 (c), 129 (c), 130 (b), 131 (c), 132 (d), 133 (c), 134 (d), 135 (b), 136 (d), 137 (a), 138 (a), 139 (a), 140 (c), 141 (a), 142 (d), 143 (d), 144 (d), 145 (d), 146 (d), 147 (d), 148 (b), 149 (c), 150 (d).

151 (d), 152 (c), 153 (d), 154 (a), 155 (d), 156 (d), 157 (c), 158 (b), 159 (c), 160 (d), 161 (d).

Part V

Miscellaneous

1 (c), 2 (a), 3 (a), 4 (b), 5 (a), 6 (b), 7 (a), 8 (d), 9 (c), 10 (b), 11 (d), 12 (c), 13 (c), 14 (b), 15 (b), 16 (c), 17 (d), 18 (b), 19 (d), 20 (c), 21 (a), 22 (b), 23 (b), 24 (c), 25 (d), 26 (d), 27 (a), 28 (a), 29 (b), 30 (b), 31 (c), 32 (d), 33 (c), 34 (d), 35 (b), 36 (d), 37 (d), 38 (d), 39 (b), 40 (d), 41 (b), 42 (d),

43 (b), 44 (c), 45 (d), 46 (d), 47 (c), 48 (c), 49 (b), 50 (c).

51 (b), 52 (a), 53 (a), 54 (c), 55 (c), 56 (a), 57 (c), 58 (b), 59 (a), 60 (b), 61 (d), 62 (a), 63 (d), 64 (c), 65 (c), 66 (a), 67 (d), 68 (a), 69 (c), 70 (b), 71 (c), 72 (b), 73 (b), 74 (c), 75 (a), 76 (b), 77 (c), 78 (d), 79 (d), 80 (c), 81 (c), 82 (d), 83 (d), 84 (c), 85 (c), 86 (a), 87 (a), 88 (d), 89 (d), 90 (b), 91 (c), 92 (b), 93 (b), 94 (c), 95 (a), 96 (c), 97 (b), 98 (b), 99 (d), 100 (d).

101 (c), 102 (b), 103 (b), 104 (d), 105 (c), 106 (b), 107 (a), 108 (a), 109 (a), 110 (a), 111 (c), 112 (c), 113 (b), 114 (d), 115 (c), 116 (a), 117 (b), 118 (c), 119 (a), 120 (d), 121 (c), 122 (a), 123 (a), 124 (d), 125 (d), 126 (a), 127 (c), 128 (d), 129 (a), 130 (b), 131 (b), 132 (d), 133 (b), 134 (c), 135 (a), 136 (d), 137 (d), 138 (c), 139 (b), 140 (a), 141 (c), 142 (d), 143 (b), 144 (a), 145 (c), 146 (b), 147 (a), 148 (c), 149 (b), 150 (c).

151 (b), 152 (d), 153 (c), 154 (a), 155 (b), 156 (d), 157 (d), 158 (b), 159 (a), 160 (d), 161 (c), 162 (b), 163 (d), 164 (b), 165 (b), 166 (d), 167 (d), 168 (a), 169 (d), 170 (d), 171 (d), 172 (c), 173 (b), 174 (c), 175 (b), 176 (d), 177 (d), 178 (a), 179 (d), 180 (d), 181 (a), 182 (a), 183 (c), 184 (b), 185 (d), 186 (a), 187 (b), 188 (b), 189 (c), 190 (d), 191 (a), 192 (c), 193 (c), 194 (c), 195 (a), 196 (d), 197 (b), 198 (b), 199 (c), 200 (b).

201 (a), 202 (b), 203 (b), 204 (a), 205 (b), 206 (d).